Successful Strategies
for Reading in the
Content Areas

2nd Edition

SHELL EDUCATION

Successful Strategies
for Reading in the Content Areas
2nd Edition
Secondary

Editor
Conni Medina

Assistant Editor
Leslie Huber, M.A.

Senior Editor
Lori Kamola, M.S.Ed.

Editor-in-Chief
Sharon Coan, M.S.Ed.

Editorial Manager
Gisela Lee, M.A.

Creative Director
Lee Aucoin

Cover Design
Neri Garcia

Interior Layout Design
Don Tran

Print Production
Kimberly Weber

Authors
TCM Staff

Publisher
Corinne Burton, M.A.Ed.

Shell Education
5301 Oceanus Drive
Huntington Beach, CA 92649
http://www.shelleducation.com
ISBN 978-1-4258-0470-1

©2008 Shell Educational Publishing, Inc.

Reprinted 2011

Learning Standards: Copyright 2004 McREL. www.mcrel.org/standards-benchmarks.

Table of Contents

Introduction

The saying "Every teacher is a teacher of reading" is well known but not always true. It is usually regarded as the task of the English or language arts teacher to guide students through the effective use of comprehension strategies as they read. Although students read in almost every subject area they study, content-area teachers typically overlook the need for guiding students through their textbook-based and trade book-based reading tasks. Comprehension strategies best serve students when they are employed across the curricula and in the context of their actual learning. It is only then that students can independently use the strategies successfully when reading. Students typically read literature or fictional stories for English or language arts, but they will spend the majority of their adulthood reading nonfiction, expository writing. The strategies that students use to comprehend literature are different from those they use for nonfiction. It is important to note that around grades four and five, educators see a drop in reading achievement. At this time, students seem to lose interest in reading independently, spend less time reading for pleasure, and struggle more to read the materials required of them at school. It is for this reason that all teachers at all levels must actively pursue ways to greatly enhance their students' abilities to understand reading material, and this can be accomplished by working directly with reading comprehension strategies.

How to Use This Book

Reading comprehension is a complex process involving interactions between the reader and the text, using multiple skills. Students need a variety of strategies to be successful readers. *Successful Strategies for Reading in the Content Areas,* 2nd Edition contains a variety of reading strategies that will help increase comprehension. This updated edition has grouped the strategies and skills to match the seven categories of strategies and skills taught in *Exploring Nonfiction: A Differentiated Content-Area Reading Program* (Teacher Created Materials Publishing 2008). An additional section, titled Developing Vocabulary, is also provided in this book. This book is divided into the following sections:

- **Monitor Comprehension** (including **Set the Purpose** and **Author's Point of View**)
- **Activate and Connect**
- **Infer Meaning**
- **Ask Questions**
- **Determine Importance** (including **Main Idea and Supporting Details, Text Structures, Text Organizers,** and **Using Parts of the Book**)
- **Visualize**
- **Summarize and Synthesize**
- **Developing Vocabulary**

Introduction

How to Use This Book *(cont.)*

Each of these eight sections contains an introduction, teaching strategies, and reproducible templates for students. Many of the teaching strategies have corresponding graphic organizers or other templates included, with page number references to direct you to the correct reproducible page. It is important to read the introduction to each section before using the strategies to understand how best to teach these important nonfiction skills. For further information, and to understand the research about reading comprehension and content-area reading, read the rest of this introduction. You will also find a Correlation to Standards chart (pages 15–16) showing the national standards to which each strategy is aligned. A CD is provided at the back of this book with all of the graphic organizers and templates in PDF format so you can print them. Most of these pages are also provided in Microsoft Word so that they can be modified. An index of these pages is provided on the CD.

This book provides a wealth of information about content-area reading strategies and skills that can be used with any nonfiction text. The strategies and skills can also be used in conjunction with *Exploring Nonfiction: A Differentiated Content-Area Reading Program* as a resource guide to support the lesson plans. Refer to the Works Cited (page 279) for a list of references used to create this book.

Research: Explicit Instruction of Reading Comprehension Strategies

If content-area teachers were asked how they improve their students' reading skills, the majority would most likely struggle to answer the question. Good teachers use many strategies to enhance students' reading comprehension, and it is helpful to identify which strategies they use in order to explain why the techniques successfully improve their students' skills. Even more important is the explicit instruction of the individual strategies, including modeling, guided practice, and independent practice. These steps ensure that students learn to independently and consistently use a wide variety of reading comprehension strategies for a broad range of reading experiences.

Teaching students the strategies to improve their comprehension is nothing new to educators. Extensive research has demonstrated that students greatly benefit from the direct instruction of reading comprehension strategies when reading a text (Duke and Pearson 2002; Block 1999; Dole, Brown, and Trathen 1996; Durkin 1978; Pressley and Afflerbach 1995, as cited by Kragler, Walker, and Martin 2005). Simply put, strategy instruction is an effective means of assisting students in improving comprehension and understanding. This book, *Successful Strategies for Reading in the Content Areas*, 2nd Edition, is designed to give content-area teachers tools for teaching reading comprehension strategies.

Introduction

Research: Which Strategies to Teach

The National Reading Panel Report (2000), commissioned by the U.S. Congress to evaluate research in the area of reading, identified a number of effective comprehension strategies. Pressley (2000) echoes these findings. These strategies include vocabulary development, prediction skills (including inference), the building of prior knowledge, think alouds, visual representations, summarization, and questioning. This book provides an explanation of these strategies and describes a number of activities that content-area teachers can incorporate into their lessons. These findings guide the selection of strategies included in *Successful Strategies for Reading in the Content Areas.*

Students also need to develop their metacognitive skills when reading and learning. Scholars agree that metacognition plays a significant role in reading comprehension (Baker and Brown 1984; Garner 1987; Mastropieri and Scruggs 1997; Paris, Wasik, and Turner 1991; Schraw 1998, as cited by Baker 2002). Research shows that teachers should foster metacognition and comprehension monitoring during comprehension instruction because students will be able to monitor and self-regulate their abilities to read. "Developing engaged readers involves helping students to become both strategic and aware of the strategies they use to read" (McCarthy, Hoffman, and Galda 1999, as cited by Baker 2002).

It is important to note that teachers should never take a "one size fits all" approach when teaching reading comprehension. Some strategies work for some students, and other strategies work for other students, just as some strategies work best with certain types of reading material, and other strategies work best with other types of reading material. The most important thing to remember when trying to improve reading comprehension in students is that the skill level, group dynamic, and makeup of the students should determine the approach to take.

Research: The Steps Involved in Explicit Instruction of Reading Comprehension Strategies

According to Duke and Pearson (2002), research supports that a balanced approach to teaching reading comprehension is more than teaching students specific reading strategies and providing opportunities to read. Teachers should begin with direct explanation and instruction of how to use the strategies so that after a series of steps, students will be able to use the strategies independently. The following are the five steps for explicit instruction of comprehension strategies:

1. **Provide an exact description of the strategy and explain when and how it should be used.** Teachers need to explain what the strategy is called, why students should use it, what it helps them understand, and how often students should use it.

2. **Provide modeling of the strategy.** Teachers should model how to use the strategy when students are in the process of reading. Students can also model the strategy while the teacher reinforces an explanation of how the strategy is being used.

3. **Provide opportunities for collaborative use of the strategy in action.** Teachers and students should work together and share their use of the strategy while they are reading.

4. **Lead guided practice sessions using the strategy, and allow for a gradual release of responsibility from the teacher to the student.** At this stage, teachers can remind students of how to use the strategy and of the steps involved, but teachers should allow students to work on the technique independently.

5. **Encourage students' independent use of the strategy.** In the final stage, teachers might gently remind students of the name of the strategy, but the students should be using the technique automatically and independently.

Duke and Pearson (2002) emphasize the importance of remembering that students need to be able to use more than one comprehension strategy to understand a reading selection. Throughout the five phases, other strategies should be referenced and modeled for the students. When working with reading materials in any content area, teachers should use the very same techniques to introduce a new learning strategy to students as they would during language arts or in an English class. Research shows that students can master the use of reading comprehension strategies when instruction follows the five steps listed above. When covering any topic, teachers must take the time to allow students to master the strategy so that they can become independent readers. Follow these steps with the strategies in this book, and students will improve their comprehension.

Introduction

Research: What Great Teachers Do

Many content-area teachers use a variety of strategies that go beyond simply answering the questions at the end of the chapter. Research shows, however, that there is a big difference between teaching reading comprehension strategies well and teaching them in a dynamic, ingenious way that motivates and excites students about reading and learning. Through research, observations, and conversations with teachers who have been successful with the direct instruction of reading comprehension strategies, Keene (2002) has identified five traits specific to outstanding and consistently effective teachers. What makes these teachers effective?

1. **They take the time to understand each strategy in their own reading.** Reading about the techniques and activities is not enough. Great teachers of reading comprehension strategies take the time to figure out how to use and understand every strategy with the texts they are reading. In doing so, they increase their own metacognitive skills and can better articulate their own thinking during reading.

2. **They incorporate reading comprehension strategy instruction into predictable daily, weekly, and monthly activities.** Effective teachers of reading comprehension strategies set goals for strategy learning and create a predictable schedule to ensure that those goals are met. These teachers also set aside time to work more intensively with small groups as needed. They also set aside time for students to reflect on their progress toward the goals they set.

3. **They ask students to apply each comprehension strategy to a wide variety of texts and text levels in different contexts.** Great teachers use beautifully written texts with challenging and profound themes that can be read in their entirety in a mini-lesson. For example, they ask students to summarize a textbook and a short story, use sensory images in poetry and expository essays, and use background knowledge to understand a biography and the letters to the editor. In order to comprehend actively and assertively, students must read texts with appropriately challenging words and concepts.

4. **They vary the size of groupings for strategy instruction.** Changing the group size and configuration helps teachers focus on different goals during comprehension-strategy instruction.

   Large groups are best for:

   - introducing a new strategy

   - modeling think alouds to show students how good readers use the strategy

   - practicing think alouds with new genres, and allowing students to share their experiences using the strategy

Research: What Great Teachers Do *(cont.)*

Small groups are best for:

- providing more intensive instruction for students who need it
- introducing gifted students to the strategy so that they can apply it independently to more challenging texts and new genres
- introducing new activities that enable students to share their thinking (maps, charts, thinking notebooks, sketches, logs, etc.)
- allowing students to discuss books and comprehension strategies without teacher involvement

Conferences are best for:

- checking a student's understanding of how to apply the strategy he or she is studying to his or her own books
- providing intensive strategy instruction for a text that may be particularly challenging to a student
- coaching a student in how he or she might reveal his or her thinking to others
- pushing a student to use a strategy to think more deeply than he or she might have imagined possible

5. **They gradually release the responsibility for the application of a comprehension strategy to the students.** Great teachers follow the steps involved in the explicit instruction of reading comprehension strategies (Duke and Pearson 2002): over several weeks, teachers provide thorough explanations of the strategy, model how to use it, allow for group work with the strategy, transition to more independent use, and then release the responsibility to the students.

By following these guidelines for the teacher and using the strategies in this book, students will be provided with rich and meaningful opportunities for comprehension instruction.

Introduction

Research: What Do Good Readers Do When They Read?

Duke and Pearson (2002) have established that good readers:

- read actively

- set goals for their reading tasks and constantly evaluate whether the text and their reading of it is meeting their goals

- preview the text prior to reading, noting the text organization and structure in order to locate the sections most relevant to their reading goals

- make predictions about what is to come in the text

- read selectively, continually making decisions about their reading process: what to read carefully, what to read quickly, what to skim, what not to read, and what to reread

- construct, revise, and question the meanings they develop as they read

- determine the meanings of unfamiliar or unknown words and concepts in the text

- draw from, compare, and integrate their prior knowledge with the material in the text

- consider the authors of the text, their style, beliefs, intentions, historical perspectives, and so on

- monitor their understanding of the text, make adjustments in their reading as necessary, and deal with inconsistencies or gaps as needed

- evaluate the text's quality and value, and interact with the text both intellectually and emotionally

- read different kinds of texts differently

- construct and revise summaries of what they have read when reading expository texts

- think about the text before, during, and after reading

- feel satisfied and productive when reading, even though comprehension is a consuming, continuous, and complex activity

Content-area teachers can easily incorporate the same techniques that language arts teachers have used for years to help students become more strategic and skilled readers and to help them comprehend the materials they encounter. Teachers will find the job of using the textbook much easier if every student has the skills of a good reader.

Opportunities for all of the activities above are provided in the strategies listed throughout this book.

Research: The Reading Process

Teachers need to understand the steps of the reading process in order to help students improve their reading comprehension skills. Content-area teachers can easily optimize the use of reading materials with students by utilizing the three-part framework of the reading process to facilitate learning. Break reading assignments into three comprehension-building steps: before reading, during reading, and after reading (Pressley 2002). It is important to note that what teachers do during each stage of the reading process is crucial to their students' learning.

Before Reading

Prior to beginning a reading assignment, engage in a variety of activities in the hopes of reducing any uncertainty involved in the reading task. These activities include generating interest in the topic, building and activating prior knowledge, and setting a purpose for reading.

Teachers who motivate students and create interest prior to assigning the reading improve their students' overall comprehension. Students who are more motivated to read are more engaged and actively involved in the process of learning than those who are not motivated. Motivated readers are also more likely to have better long-term recall of what they read.

Teachers can motivate students by assessing their prior knowledge. Knowing students' background knowledge on a topic makes it easier to build on and activate that knowledge during reading. The mind holds information in the form of frameworks called *schemata*, and as we learn new information, we store it in a framework of what we already know. Teachers who build on and activate students' prior knowledge before reading prepare students to more efficiently comprehend the material that they will be reading.

Prior to reading, teachers should prepare students to read by setting a purpose for the reading task. There are a number of different purposes a student can have for a reading assignment: predict what will happen, learn new vocabulary, summarize the information, evaluate the author's point of view, and so on. Students need to know what their purpose is as they read because it helps them to focus their efforts. In doing so, teachers can guide the students' search for meaning as they read.

Teachers should also take the time to introduce key concepts and vocabulary prior to reading. In doing so, they help the students read the selection more fluently, with greater automaticity, and with greater comprehension—all of which lead to greater recall of the information.

Finally, teachers should establish in their students a metacognitive awareness for the task of reading. Students should be prompted to be aware of what they are thinking and doing as they are reading. Developing metacognitive awareness allows students to better understand the strategies necessary for effective learning. It also enables students to take control of their own learning, making them more independent readers and learners.

Introduction

Research: The Reading Process *(cont.)*

During Reading

During reading, students are actively reading text aloud or silently. During this stage of the reading process, students are engaged in answering questions (either self-generated or teacher-generated), monitoring their comprehension of the text, clarifying the purpose of reading, visualizing the information, and building connections.

Most often, students are engaged in answering questions while they read. Proficient readers self-question as they read to make sure they understand the reading material. In addition, students search for the answers to questions they may have generated prior to reading. As students process the text, they begin to infer what the author intended, and they begin to generalize about the specific details in the information provided. They also look for support for the predictions they have made.

Students are involved in monitoring and regulating their reading abilities while they are actively reading. If a section of the text is confusing, students need to know that they can reread the section, use fix-up strategies to help them understand what they are puzzled by, or adjust the speed of reading to suit their purposes and the difficulty of the text. Thus, students must monitor their own reading strategies and make modifications as needed.

In addition to monitoring their reading abilities, students are also figuring out words as they actively read. If they do not know what a word means, they use the context clues or word parts to decode the meaning of the word. As students attend to vocabulary needs, they also observe the text structure and features as they read, which helps them organize the new information.

During reading, teachers can focus students' attention on the objectives of the reading task. Students may adjust their purposes for reading based on the information they are reading and on their prior knowledge.

Proficient readers actively work to create images in their minds that represent the concepts in the reading material. Teachers should engage the students in creating mental images to help them comprehend the material as they are reading. This promotes greater recall of the information and engages the students in the reading process.

While students are reading, they are in the process of connecting the new information they are learning to their existing schemata. Therefore, teachers should be actively involved in helping students make connections between what they already know and what they are learning. This prepares them for the synthesis of the information. Teachers can be instrumental in helping students relate to the material.

Research: The Reading Process *(cont.)*

After Reading

Students expand their understanding of the material after reading the text. During the final stage of the reading process, students build connections among the bits of information that they have read, enabling them to deepen their understanding and reflect on what they have learned.

After reading, students need the teacher to guide them through follow-up exercises so they can reflect on what they have read. During reflection, students can contemplate the new information, clarify new ideas, refine their thinking, and connect what they have learned to other ideas to synthesize the new information. Teachers should spend time revisiting the text with students to demonstrate that the reading experience is not a single event.

Also, students generally find the main idea and distinguish the most important ideas from less important ideas. This enables them to prioritize and summarize what they have read.

After reading, teachers generally assess what students have learned. Students answer questions about what they have learned, and teachers generally use their answers to determine whether the students can move on or need additional instruction. Teachers can take advantage of additional activities for after reading to deepen students' comprehension of the text.

After students have read, they are able to engage in higher-level thinking tasks. Students can use critical thinking to evaluate the quality or validity of the material, or they can synthesize what they have learned by integrating their new knowledge with their prior knowledge. They can also analyze what they have read by closely examining the text characteristics specific to the genre.

Introduction

Correlation to Standards

The No Child Left Behind (NCLB) legislation mandates that all states adopt academic standards that identify the skills students will learn in kindergarten through grade 12. While many states had already adopted academic standards prior to NCLB, the legislation set requirements to ensure the standards were detailed and comprehensive.

Standards are designed to focus instruction and guide adoption of curricula. Standards are statements that describe the criteria necessary for students to meet specific academic goals. They define the knowledge, skills, and content students should acquire at each level. Standards are also used to develop standardized tests to evaluate students' academic progress.

In many states today, teachers are required to demonstrate how their lessons meet state standards. State standards are used in the development of Shell Education products, so educators can be assured that they meet the academic requirements of each state.

How to Find Your State Correlations

Shell Education is committed to producing educational materials that are research- and standards-based. In this effort, all products are correlated to the academic standards of the 50 states, the District of Columbia, and the Department of Defense Dependent Schools. A correlation report customized for your state can be printed directly from the following website: **http://www.shelleducation.com**. If you require assistance in printing correlation reports, please contact Customer Service at 1-877-777-3450.

McREL Compendium

Shell Education uses the Mid-continent Research for Education and Learning (McREL) Compendium to create standards correlations. Each year, McREL analyzes state standards and revises the compendium. By following this procedure, McREL is able to produce a general compilation of national standards.

Each reading comprehension strategy assessed in this book is based on one or more McREL content standards. The chart on pages 15–16 shows the McREL standards that correlate to each strategy provided in the book.

Introduction

Correlation to Standards *(cont.)*

Standard/Objective	Page (Strategy)
5.1—Establishes and adjusts purposes for reading (e.g., to understand, interpret, enjoy, solve problems, predict outcomes, answer a specific question, form an opinion, skim for facts; to discover models for own writing)	22(1, 2, 3, 4); 23(5, 6, 7, 8); 24(9, 10, 11); 25(12, 13, 14); 46(11); 47(12); 167(3, 4); 168(5, 6, 7); 169(8, 9, 10); 185(1, 2); 189(10); 245(7)
5.3—Uses a variety of strategies to extend reading vocabulary (e.g., uses analogies, idioms, similes, and metaphors to infer the meaning of literal and figurative phrases; uses definition, restatement, example, comparison and contrast to verify word meanings; identifies shades of meaning; knows denotative and connotative meanings; knows vocabulary related to different content areas and current events; uses rhyming dictionaries, classification books, etymological dictionaries)	67(9); 168(5); 211(5); 245(9); 264(1); 265(2, 3, 4); 266(5, 6, 7); 267(8, 9, 10, 11)
5.4—Uses specific strategies to clear up confusing parts of a text (e.g., pauses, rereads the text, consults another source, represents abstract information as mental pictures, draws upon background knowledge, asks for help)	43(4); 65(4); 67(5, 8, 9); 68(12); 88(11); 111(6, 8); 112(10, 11); 166(2); 209(1, 2); 210(3, 4); 211(5); 213(13, 14, 15); 239(1); 267(8)
5.5—Understands specific devices an author uses to accomplish his or her purpose (e.g., persuasive techniques, style, word choice, language structure)	23(6, 8); 24(9); 25(13, 14); 42(1); 43(2, 3, 4); 44(5, 6); 45(7, 8, 9, 10); 46(11); 47(12); 170(11, 12); 189(10); 240(2); 265(2)
5.6—Reflects on what has been learned after reading and formulates ideas, opinions, and personal responses to texts	22(1, 2, 4); 25(12); 64(1); 65(3); 67(6, 7); 68(10, 12); 87(2, 3, 4, 5, 6); 109(4); 111(7); 112(9); 132(2); 169(9, 10); 170(13); 185(1, 2); 186(3); 187(4, 5, 6); 188(7, 8); 189(11); 243(4); 266(5)

Introduction

Correlation to Standards *(cont.)*

Standard/Objective	Page (Strategy)
7.2—Knows the defining characteristics of a variety of informational texts (e.g., electronic texts; textbooks; biographical sketches; letters; diaries; directions; procedures; magazines; essays; primary source historical documents; editorials; news stories; periodicals; bus routes; catalogs; technical directions; consumer, workplace, and public documents)	23(5); 88(10); 132(3); 168(6, 7); 169(8); 170(11, 12, 13); 187(4, 5, 6); 188(7, 8); 189(11); 267(9)
7.3—Summarizes and paraphrases information in texts (e.g., arranges information in chronological, logical, or sequential order; conveys main ideas, critical details, and underlying meaning; uses own words or quoted materials; preserves author's perspective and voice)	24(11); 43(3); 68(10); 131(1); 132(2, 3); 133(4, 5); 134(6, 7, 8, 9); 135(10, 11); 150(1, 2, 3, 4); 151(5, 6, 7); 152(8, 9, 10, 11); 188(9); 211(6, 7, 8); 212(9, 10, 11, 12); 213(13, 14, 15); 239(1); 240(2); 241(3); 243(4, 5); 244(6); 245(7, 8, 9, 10, 11); 266(6)
7.4—Uses new information to adjust and extend personal knowledge base	24(10); 45(10); 64(1, 2); 65(3, 4); 68(11); 88(7, 8, 9); 109(2, 3); 134(7, 8, 9); 135(10, 11); 150(1, 2, 3, 4); 151(5, 6, 7); 152(8, 9, 10, 11); 209(1, 2); 210(3, 4); 211(6, 7, 8); 212(9, 10, 11, 12); 241(3); 244(6); 264(1); 265(3); 266(7); 267(10, 11)
7.5—Draws conclusions and makes inferences based on explicit and implicit information in texts	23(7); 45(9); 67(5, 6, 7, 8); 86(1); 87(2, 3, 4, 5, 6); 88(7, 8, 9, 10, 11); 109(1); 110(5); 133(4); 166(1, 2); 167(4); 188(9)
7.6—Differentiates between fact and opinion in informational texts	43(2); 44(5, 6); 45(7, 8)
8.2—Asks questions to seek elaboration and clarification of ideas	22(3, 4); 42(1); 64(2); 86(1), 109(1, 2, 3, 4); 110(5); 111(6, 7, 8); 112(9, 10, 11); 113(12, 13, 14); 131(1); 133(5); 134(6); 167(3); 186(3); 243(5); 245(11); 265(4)

Monitor Comprehension

Monitor Comprehension— Set the Purpose

Introduction

All meaningful reading needs a purpose. Even without explicitly or consciously stating why they are reading, strategic readers survey the reading material and assess why they are reading it. This technique helps to establish how to read a particular piece of writing. The traditional setting for teachers to provide students with a purpose for reading is when giving an assignment. Although helpful to some students, this method does not allow students to determine their own purposes for reading. Consequently, less proficient readers wait until the purpose is set for them and then read only to obtain that small piece of specified information. Very little actual learning takes place in this setting.

The process of reading should begin before a book is opened. Teachers can help students become effective, systematic readers by teaching strategies that reinforce the purpose for reading a piece of nonfiction text.

Stating the Purpose for Reading

Most of the time we give students their purpose for reading. We tell them that they will be reading to learn about a particular topic, such as the Civil War in social studies, the French Impressionists in art, or habitats for various animals in science. Students must be able to identify their own purposes for reading as well as read for an assigned purpose. Expose students to the idea that people read for different purposes, which include reading to:

- be entertained, informed, or persuaded

- learn how to do something

- analyze the author

- reflect upon and extend personal experience and prior knowledge

- generate questions for further research about the topic or concept

- gather information for a discussion

It is important that students keep their purpose in mind while reading so that they can sort and organize the new information, connect it to their purpose for reading, and articulate and justify how the information they have gained helps them achieve their purpose for reading.

Choosing Appropriate Materials to Read

Once students know and understand their purpose for reading, they should be given opportunities to select texts that will help them achieve their purpose. Students need to be taught how to preview the text, skim for main ideas and supporting details, make note of headings and subheadings, critically analyze graphic features, and carefully read the back cover, inside cover, and any other surface information that will help them determine the appropriateness of the text.

Monitor Comprehension— Set the Purpose

Using Appropriate Strategies for Different Purposes

Being able to set the purpose for reading is a vital first step toward developing strategic reading skills. Students need to be able to skim and scan effectively to locate information quickly. They need to be able to read carefully in order to gain full comprehension and read critically in order to analyze or interpret the author's intent. These are just some of the skills that students need to acquire in order to meet the purpose for reading. Make sure to expose students to text coding, double-entry journals, partner journals, discussion techniques, and graphic organizers in order for them to read for entertainment, information, critical analysis of the author, or whatever their purpose may be.

Enjoying Nonfiction Text

Reading nonfiction opens a world of opportunities for learning about many diverse and interesting topics. Having students conduct I-Search projects in which they identify a topic of interest to them, brainstorm questions related to the topic, and then conduct research can expose them to a wealth of nonfiction reading. Make sure to teach students to analyze text features including charts, graphs, diagrams, and maps and their relationship to the author's purpose.

Solving Problems

One of the most compelling purposes for reading is to solve a problem. Have students generate topics of interest and problems that concern them. These problems can be related to local, state, national, or international issues. Have students read from a multitude of nonfiction sources in order to solve the problem or at least to gain information to understand the issue more completely.

Forming an Opinion

Another purpose for reading that is highly motivating for students is reading to form an opinion. Students have their own ideas about many topics. Teachers need to coach students in researching different viewpoints to form an intelligent opinion, one that they can back up with statistics, details, and more specific information.

Skimming for Facts

When students have identified a motivating and focused purpose for reading, model how to skim for facts. Skimming involves reading chapter headings and subheadings, the chapter introductions and summaries, and the questions, if any, at the end of a chapter. Next, read any information that is given special attention by different typeface, different color print, plus graphics and their captions. Students must be able to read to gain information from a multitude of sources. To tackle as many sources as possible, students will need to skim information quickly, discern which information matches their purpose for reading, and decide which information needs careful study.

Monitor Comprehension— Set the Purpose

Discovering Models

As students are reading, make sure to emphasize that they are also writers. Students must understand that when they read, they should also be thinking about how the author's words affect them. This will give them a better understanding of how to affect the readers of their own writing. Teach them to be critical readers who are able to identify organizational patterns in text, text features, key vocabulary, and rhetorical techniques.

Establishing and Adjusting Purposes

When students conduct their own research, give them guidance in selecting a topic of interest to them. Then ask them to formulate a research question that, in essence, will establish their purpose for reading. As they read and do research, have students adjust their purpose for reading by refining and revising their initial research question. Inform them that professional researchers follow the same process. By establishing and adjusting purposes for reading, students will learn how to be strategic thinkers and problem solvers while reading.

Using Characteristics to Choose Nonfiction Material

Often, teachers will present students with characteristics for selecting their nonfiction reading material. As an alternative, allow students to generate their own characteristics or criteria for choosing nonfiction material; this will help build independence in students. Examples may include criteria that the material connects to a specific topic, contains text features, has multiple viewpoints, and is highly engaging in physical appearance and presentation. Have students discuss these characteristics and evaluate whether the nonfiction material that they have selected has these characteristics.

Using Strategies Independently

Model how students should set their own purposes for reading. Start at the school library and allow them to browse through books at least once every three weeks and to select books for enjoyment. Once students have selected books, have them share with the class what they chose and why. Allow them to choose fiction and nonfiction. Expose students to a variety of techniques for book selection: examining the book jacket and the inside cover, reading about the author, scanning the chapter titles, reading the first few paragraphs, etc. Make book selection a celebration of independent choice.

Monitor Comprehension— Set the Purpose

Strategy 1: Evaluating Purpose

Allow students to select books of their choice and have them identify many purposes for reading those books. Have students complete the graphic organizer Evaluating Purpose (page 26) by recording their purposes, identifying whether they achieved their purposes, and writing a brief explanation that evaluates why they did or did not achieve their purpose. Have students compare their evaluations with a partner. (Standards 5.1, 5.6)

Strategy 2: Text Coding for Purpose

A simple coding strategy that will help students read to achieve their purpose is identified on the Text Coding for Purpose activity (page 27). As students are reading, have them mark the text with a "P!" to note a strong connection to purpose and a "P" to note some connection to purpose. (If students are not allowed to write directly in the text, have them use sticky notes.) When they finish reading the nonfiction text, have them record the text information that corresponds with the code that they chose in the left column of the chart and then write a reaction to the selected text in the right column. Have students reflect on how the information connects to their purpose for reading and their prior knowledge of the subject. (Standards 5.1, 5.6)

Strategy 3: Question/Answer

Begin by having students identify their purpose for reading. Then lead them in generating a list of prereading questions that will help them achieve their purpose. For example, if students are reading about the history of baseball and their purpose is to understand the history and know why it's important to the sport today, they may generate several questions, such as 1) Who invented the game of baseball? 2) Where was it invented? 3) What were the initial reactions to the game? 4) How do people react to the game today? Students should write their questions in the left column of the Question/Answer chart (page 28) and record the answers in the right column as they find them in the text. Remind students that in order to answer some of the questions, they may need to make inferences. When they have finished their charts, have them reflect on how the process of questioning helped them achieve their purpose for reading. (Standards 5.1, 8.2)

Strategy 4: Question/Answer/Opinion

Follow the same procedures as the Question/Answer strategy. However, this time have students also write brief opinions about the topics they researched. Some helpful sentence starters include:

- I was surprised to learn that…
- This information confirms what I knew about…
- I agree/disagree because…

Use the Question/Answer/Opinion graphic organizer on page 29 for this strategy. (Standards 5.1, 5.6, 8.2)

Monitor Comprehension— Set the Purpose

Strategy 5: Examining Multiple Texts

A great way to motivate students to examine multiple texts is to present them with a purpose for reading. If possible, take students to the school library to select books to achieve their purpose. For example, imagine that the students' purpose for reading is to learn about the solar system. Have them use the Examining Multiple Texts activity (page 30) to preview three different texts and to think about how the text would help them achieve their purpose for reading. Instruct students to select the best text and to read more deeply to acquire the necessary information. (Standards 5.1, 7.2)

Strategy 6: Author and Me Analysis

It is important for students to understand that they read for a variety of purposes, but authors also write for a variety of purposes. Use the Author and Me Analysis activity (page 31) to have students identify their purpose and the author's purpose. Chances are that if the student is reading to be informed, the author was writing to provide the reader with information. As students are reading, have them record important information in the left column and make connections to their purpose for reading and the author's purpose for writing in the remaining columns. An additional activity, Purpose and Analyzing the Author (page 32), can be used for this strategy. (Standards 5.1, 5.5)

Strategy 7: Purpose and Solving Problems

One of the most important things for educators to do is teach students that they can read in order to solve problems and important issues. It is vital for students to know that text contains information that is highly interesting and motivating. Expose students to interesting, engaging text as often as possible. Have them use the Purpose and Solving Problems activity (page 33) to record problems and issues that they encounter in their reading in the left column. Then have students explain in the right column whether they better understand the issue and how they will act upon it. To create an educational atmosphere that sends the message that reading is fun, make sure to have many nonfiction materials available to students. (Standards 5.1, 7.5)

Strategy 8: Reading and Skimming for Facts

In content-area classrooms, one of the most common purposes for reading is to be informed. Create an atmosphere where learning is valuable and informational text is viewed as intriguing. Distribute the Reading and Skimming for Facts activity (page 34) and have students record facts and details in the left column and write a reaction in the right column. Make sure students think about why the author wanted them to learn the information, why the information will be valuable to them, and any further questions they may have. (Standards 5.1, 5.5)

Monitor Comprehension— Set the Purpose

Strategy 9: Purpose and Being Persuaded

We are surrounded by text that is intended to be persuasive. Have students read a variety of texts that are persuasive and show them how to analyze the author's use of rhetorical language, examples, and appeals to the audience to make his or her argument convincing. Distribute the Purpose and Being Persuaded activity (page 35) and have students record text information that is persuasive. In the right column, have them write a reaction in which they think about the choices that the author made and why those choices made the text convincing. Allow students to identify ideas with which they disagree or text that is not convincing. (Standards 5.1, 5.5)

Strategy 10: Purpose and Extending Prior Knowledge

Extending and enriching students' prior knowledge about a subject can be very beneficial in deepening their understanding. As an introductory activity to reading information on a topic that is already familiar to students, have them sit in a circle. In round-robin fashion, ask them to share something they know about the topic or concept. As a variation, begin with a KWL chart to help them identify their prior knowledge. Distribute the Purpose and Extending Prior Knowledge activity (page 36) and have students record in the left column information that connects to what they already know as they are reading. In the right column, have them write a reaction in which they connect this information to their personal experiences and/or prior knowledge. Encourage students to write about information that surprised them or confirmed what they already knew. (Standards 5.1, 7.4)

Strategy 11: Purpose and Following Directions

Students will encounter sets of instructions, recipes, and rule books throughout their lives and need to know how to read critically in order to create a product or learn how to do something. Have students identify something that they would like to learn how to do or make. Take them to the school library and allow them to find resources that fit their learning objectives. Distribute the Purpose and Following Directions activity (page 37), and have them paraphrase the step-by-step instructions in the left column. Have them write a reaction in the right side of the column by analyzing the clarity of the instructions, the effectiveness of the graphic organizers, or identifying any further questions they have based on areas of confusion. (Standards 5.1, 7.3)

Monitor Comprehension— Set the Purpose

Strategy 12: Partnered Reading

Have students read for a common purpose and gather text information to achieve their purpose with the Partnered Reading activity (page 38). Then have them discuss the text and write a reaction about how the information connects to what they already know and whether they have any further questions. (Standards 5.1, 5.6)

Strategy 13: Skimming for Purpose

Skimming focuses on general information and is an important skill to utilize when students are learning to take effective notes. Skimming involves reading chapter headings and subheadings, chapter introductions and summaries, and questions, if any, at the end of a chapter. Next, read any information that is given special attention by different typeface, different print color, plus graphics and their captions. (Standards 5.1, 5.5)

Strategy 14: Selective Reading Guide

Prepare a Selective Reading Guide (Cunningham and Shablak 1975) to teach students to use their textbooks as a resource rather than a book to be read from cover to cover. This strategy is particularly effective with struggling or reluctant readers because it lets them know which information is most essential and helps them understand how to establish a purpose for reading. (Standards 5.1, 5.5)

Here is an example:

---

page 186

Paragraphs 1 & 2—Introduce the section. Read them quickly.

Paragraphs 3 & 4—Define an ocean and its importance to our planet. Know the names of the world's oceans and their locations on a world map or globe.

---

page 187

Paragraph 1—Based on the information in this paragraph, make a list of the world's five oceans in order of their size.

Paragraphs 2 & 3—Pay attention to differences in the oceans' average temperatures and their effect on the world's weather.

Paragraphs 4 & 5—Skim these paragraphs.

Monitor Comprehension— Set the Purpose

Evaluating Purpose

Directions: Identify your purposes for reading. Be very specific. For example, if your purpose is to be informed, identify specifically the topics about which you would like to be informed. After reading, determine whether you achieved your purpose and write an explanation.

My purposes for reading	Did I achieve my purpose?	Explanation
	YES NO	
	YES NO	
	YES NO	
	YES NO	
	YES NO	
	YES NO	

Monitor Comprehension—
Set the Purpose

Text Coding for Purpose

Directions: Before reading, identify your purpose. As you are reading, mark in the text or on a sticky note using the codes below. Then record in the left column the text that corresponds with the codes. In the right column, use the guiding questions to write a reaction.

P! = Strong connection to purpose for reading

P = Some connection to purpose for reading

Purpose for reading: _____

_____

Text information that connects to my purpose for reading	Reaction: How does this information connect to your purpose for reading? How does this information connect to your prior knowledge of the subject? What further questions do you have?

Monitor Comprehension—
Set the Purpose

Question/Answer

Directions: Before reading, record questions that will help you achieve your purpose for reading. As you read, record the answers to your questions.

My purpose for reading: _____

My questions about the text information	Answers

How did questioning help me achieve my purpose for reading?

_____

_____

_____

_____

Monitor Comprehension—
Set the Purpose

Question/Answer/Opinion

Directions: Before reading, use this chart to record questions that will help you achieve your purpose for reading. Record the answers as you read. After reading, write an opinion about the text information you found.

My purpose for reading: _____

_____

My questions	Answers	My opinions

Monitor Comprehension— Set the Purpose

Examining Multiple Texts

Directions: Look through three different texts. Establish your purpose for reading. Compare each text and determine how each text will help you achieve your purpose for reading.

Purpose for Reading: _____

_____

Text #1: _____

Information gained through previewing (topics, concepts, ideas): _____

_____

_____

How will this text help me achieve my purpose for reading? _____

_____

_____

_____

Text #2: _____

Information gained through previewing (topics, concepts, ideas): _____

_____

_____

How will this text help me achieve my purpose for reading? _____

_____

_____

Text #3: _____

Information gained through previewing (topics, concepts, ideas): _____

_____

_____

How will this text help me achieve my purpose for reading? _____

_____

_____

Monitor Comprehension— Set the Purpose

Author and Me Analysis

Directions: Compare your purpose for reading with the author's purpose for writing.

My purpose for reading: _____

_____

The author's purpose for writing: _____

_____

Important information	How does this information connect to the author's purpose?	How does this information connect to my purpose for reading?

Monitor Comprehension—
Set the Purpose

Purpose and Analyzing the Author

Directions: Your purpose for reading is to analyze the author. As you read, record text information on the left side of the chart that reveals the author's purpose. On the right side of the chart, use the guiding questions to write a reaction.

Title of the text: _____

Text information that reveals the author's purpose	Reaction: What does the author want me to learn about the topic? What language choices does the author use to achieve his or her purpose? What graphic features does the author include to achieve his or her purpose? How do the author's examples achieve his or her purpose?

Monitor Comprehension—
Set the Purpose

Purpose and Solving Problems

Directions: Your purpose for reading is to solve a problem. As you read, record text information on the left side of the chart that helps you identify the problem. On the right side of the chart, use the guiding questions to write a reaction.

Research question: _____

_____

Text that helps me identify the problem	Reaction: How does the text make me feel? How does the information help me better understand the problem? What further problems or issues can I think of after reading?

Monitor Comprehension—
Set the Purpose

Reading and Skimming for Facts

Directions: Your purpose for reading is to skim for facts and determine which facts are important. As you read, record text information on the left side of the chart that is informative, factual, or helps you learn about the topic or concept. On the right side of the chart, use the guiding questions to write a reaction.

Title of the text: _____

Text information that helps me learn about the topic or concept	Reaction: What was the most important information I learned? What were the most important facts or details I learned? Why? What did the author want me to learn from this information? Do I have any further questions?

Monitor Comprehension—
Set the Purpose

Purpose and Being Persuaded

Directions: Your purpose for reading is to be persuaded about the topic. As you read, record text information on the left side of the chart that is convincing and persuasive. On the right side of the chart, use the guiding questions to write a reaction.

Title of the text: _____

Text information that is convincing or persuasive (Remember to carefully examine the content of the text and the graphic features.)	Reaction: Why is this information persuasive? Does the author use language, examples, or graphic features that are particularly convincing? Explain. Will I take action as a result of this information? How could the information be more persuasive?

Is there any part of the text that you don't agree with or that is not convincing? Explain.

_____

_____

_____

Monitor Comprehension—
Set the Purpose

Purpose and Extending Prior Knowledge

Directions: Your purpose for reading is to extend your prior knowledge. As you read, record text information on the left side of the chart that connects to what you already know about the topic or concept. On the right side of the chart, use the guiding questions to write a reaction.

Title of the text: _____

Text information that connects to my personal experience or prior knowledge of the topic or concept	Reaction: How does this information connect to my personal experience or prior knowledge? Does this information surprise me or confirm what I already know? Do I agree or disagree with any of the information? Explain.

Monitor Comprehension—
Set the Purpose

Purpose and Following Directions

Directions: Your purpose for reading is to follow directions. As you read, record text information on the left side of the chart that teaches you how to achieve your task. On the right side of the chart, use the guiding questions to write a reaction.

Title of the text: _____

Text information that shows the step-by-step nature of the directions	Reaction: Are the instructions clear? How could the instructions be clearer? How could the author have included more graphic features to clarify the instructions? What questions do I still have? Based on what I learned, could I teach someone else how to achieve the task?

Monitor Comprehension—
Set the Purpose

Partnered Reading

Directions: Both you and your partner have the same purpose for reading. Gather information to achieve your purpose and then react to the information.

Purpose for reading: _____

Partner #1: Text information that helps achieve the purpose for reading:	**Partner #2:** Text information that helps achieve the purpose for reading:
Partner #1: Reaction (How does this information connect to what I already know about the topic? What further questions do I have?)	**Partner #2:** Reaction (How does this information connect to what I already know about the topic? What further questions do I have?)

Monitor Comprehension— Author's Point of View

Introduction

The concept of the author's viewpoint differs between fiction and nonfiction. In fiction, the author creates a character, or even multiple characters, who tells the story through a created point of view. Fiction is subjective, as the characters, setting, and plot work together to evoke feelings and mood in the reader.

On the other hand, a nonfiction author's viewpoint exists on more of a continuum. A nonfiction work may be objective or subjective, neutral or biased, depending on the purpose, intended audience, and type of text. At one end of the continuum are materials that convey information, such as news articles, instruction manuals, and reference books. These materials are objective and are usually written in third person. The author's personal viewpoint is omitted and is considered nonessential. At the other end of the continuum are subjective texts, such as essays, memoirs, and autobiographies in which the author's viewpoint is central to the work. Editorials are the midpoint of the continuum. Based on facts in current events, editorials contain the author's commentary on contemporary social patterns and political issues.

Of course, many texts combine both fact and opinion, either intentionally or unintentionally. For example, cookbooks are nonfiction, but cooks may differ considerably in their approaches to cooking. History books, on the other hand, are supposed to be objective, but they often contain bias. The victors in a battle, for example, may seem righteous while the viewpoints of others involved in the battle are not even discussed. For anyone who pays attention to medical news, there is bias as well; witness the back-and-forth clamor over low- versus high-carbohydrate diets or the risks and benefits of vitamin C.

Teaching students to recognize bias and to separate fact from opinion is one of the first steps in helping them recognize that nonfiction is not always "the truth." They also need to understand that fact and opinion can be found in the same piece of writing. Teaching students to develop healthy skepticism and to question the source of information is essential. The ability to form opinions and to express them requires critical thinking. Some students will be more ready than others to read critically for point of view, but this skill can be taught.

The Difference between Fact and Opinion

When reading in the content areas, students must understand how authors use fact and opinion to achieve their purposes. Authors write nonfiction to inform, persuade, or entertain. When they choose their examples and supporting details in informational and persuasive writing, authors use a blend of facts and opinions.

Monitor Comprehension— Author's Point of View

The Difference between Fact and Opinion *(cont.)*

Begin by presenting students with pairs of sentences, one reflecting fact and one reflecting opinion, like those shown below. Thereafter, use sentence pairs that relate to a text you are currently reading in class.

Examples

Roses need specific amounts of nitrogen, water, and sun to produce the best blooms.

All roses are most lovely when they have just the right amount of water, soil, and sun.

To be nutritious, school cafeteria menus need to include the five food groups.

When meat is included in the school cafeteria menu, it can no longer be nutritious.

Point out to students that facts are difficult to dispute. Roses do have very specific requirements; they cannot grow in the shade, for example. Opinions, on the other hand, can be debated. For example, roses may have rust and produce sparse flowers no matter how exacting the gardener may be, so not all roses are "lovely." Discuss the second pair of sentences in the same way. The first sentence comes from well-accepted, established research; the second comes from what appears to be a vegetarian author who does not see the value of meat as part of the school menu. Opinions provoke debate; without support, they do not hold up to examination in the way that facts do. Of course, facts can be disputed as well, but usually investigation is required in order to change a fact. An opinion can be changed in an instant.

You can extend this activity by looking at paragraphs from several different sources, even seemingly objective ones such as front-page newspaper stories, and reading them sentence by sentence to discover fact and opinion. Tell students that they will learn to think for themselves by questioning and analyzing what they read.

To demonstrate the investigation of facts, have students write 10 sentences, half of them true and half false, based on a social studies or science text that the class is currently reading. Ask them to exchange papers with a classmate. The classmate must then determine which are facts, citing page and paragraph numbers in the text. They should then correct any false sentences so that they read as facts based on the text.

Monitor Comprehension— Author's Point of View

Determining Point of View

Much of nonfiction writing is impersonal and, therefore, written in third person. This point of view is the most objective, the one that best conveys facts without the intrusion of the author's thoughts, feelings, and opinions. But two other points of view—first and second—are used in different texts and for different purposes in nonfiction. For example:

- **First person:** Editorials, essays, autobiographies, original-source material (diaries, letters, etc.), reviews, eyewitness accounts; text that conveys immediacy. Authors use first-person pronouns—I, me, my, we, us, our.
- **Second person:** Advertising, campaign propaganda, brochures; text with which the author wants the reader to identify. Authors use second-person pronouns—you, your, yours.
- **Third person:** Descriptions, chronologies, research, reports, news items, in-depth articles. Authors use third-person pronouns—he, she, they, him, her, them, his, hers, their, theirs.

Make a habit of asking students to identify the point of view whenever they begin reading a new piece of nonfiction. Ask them why the author may have chosen this point of view and how the piece would be changed if it were written from a different point of view.

Making Sense of the Author's Word Choice

The words in the text should reflect an author's knowledge of the topic with the intent of informing the reader. Informational writers use rhetorical questions, incorporate figurative language when appropriate, and vary their sentence length and structure. Most authors not only want the information to be accessible, but also want to achieve their purpose by allowing the reader to "enter" into the text comfortably. Authors do this by making the word choice and language interesting, compelling, and appropriate to the audience's knowledge level, age, and experiences. Also, remind students to notice the denotation and connotation of words when they examine an author's language for bias.

Using Context to Determine Author's Viewpoint

It is important for readers to understand that there is a context in which the author's viewpoint is created. Encourage students to use the following questions to determine the context: When and where do the events in the article take place? What are other events connected to the topic? What is the author's connection to the topic?

Sometimes context is irrelevant or difficult to determine. When working with many different kinds of text, it may be challenging to get information about the author and his or her connection to the topic. However, when appropriate, provide students with information about the author and his or her connection to the topic and any other outside information relevant to the topic that might help determine any bias.

Monitor Comprehension—Author's Point of View

Evaluating the Author's Viewpoint

Some strategies presented in this section are intended to guide you in helping students recognize and evaluate the author's point of view. The following questions may help students evaluate the author's effectiveness: Did the author use an appropriate balance of facts and opinions? Is the author's bias toward the topic apparent? What information should the author have added? What information could the author delete? What questions do you have for the author?

Strategy 1: Question/Answer Role-Playing

Assign students the role of the reader while you assume the role of the author. After students read a text together, have them engage in a spontaneous question/answer period. A reader will ask the "author" about his or her choices of organizational structure, word selection, examples, and language. The author will ask the readers questions pertaining to clarity of ideas and language. The author may also ask what the readers want to know more about. This process may be difficult at first because students will have to become familiar with using the inferring skills necessary to complete this activity. Model a dialogue in which you assume the role of author and a student assumes the role of the reader. (Standards 5.5, 8.2)

The following example could occur after reading a text on Helen Keller:

Student/Reader: I thought your biography of Helen Keller was informative and interesting. How did you choose the organization of your writing?

Teacher/Author: I figured that readers would want to know about her life from start to finish, so I wrote the story chronologically from her birth to her death.

Student/Reader: You spent a lot of time writing about Annie Sullivan. That made me realize how important she was to Helen Keller.

Teacher/Author: I wanted to convey that exact idea. Annie Sullivan was responsible for teaching Helen to communicate with the world. She really changed her entire life.

Student/Reader: When you said that Helen was determined to see and hear in any way possible, what did you mean? I thought she was blind and deaf and could not see or hear.

Teacher/Author: I wrote that because she really learned to see and hear things in her own way. She might not have been able to do those things the way we can, but she learned other ways of communicating that made it possible for her to understand the world around her.

Student/Reader: The pictures of her traveling around the world and sharing her story made me understand how brave she really was.

Teacher/Author: I thought it was important to show real pictures of her. People tend to forget she was a real person because they hear so many things about her life.

Monitor Comprehension— Author's Point of View

Strategy 2: Fact vs. Opinion

Have students read text that contains a blend of facts and opinions. Pair them with partners to generate a quiz that contains only questions about the facts in the text. Have them switch papers with another pair and answer the fact-based questions. Then give them a chart with three categories: facts, the author's opinion of the topic, my opinion of the topic. Have them complete the chart and then discuss with them the differences between fact and opinion, as well as the similarities and differences between their opinions and the author's opinions. As a variation, have students work with a partner and use the Fact vs. Opinion Partner Chart (page 48) to record facts from the text and the opinions of each partner. Make sure to emphasize that authors use a blend of facts and opinions intentionally to achieve their purpose. Also, have them practice separating fact from opinion by completing the Separating Fact from Opinion activity (page 49). (Standards 5.5, 7.6)

Strategy 3: Point of View

Students may need practice in recognizing first-, second-, and third-person point of view. The Point of View activity (page 50) provides students with more information about the three points of view and gives them practice with rewriting and changing a point of view and writing from one point of view. (Standards 5.5, 7.3)

Strategy 4: Biased and Nonbiased Storytelling

With students sitting in a large circle, tell two simple stories about your morning. The first story should include language that is calm, reasonable, and non-biased. Present only the facts. The second story should involve the same information but should include overly emotional, biased judgments about the morning's events. Then give students a topic, such as "our school hallways" or "summertime." Going around the circle, have each student tell one non-biased sentence about the topic. Then go around again with each telling one sentence that is overly emotional and judgmental. Discuss the importance of using reasonable, rational language and examples when presenting information in order to prove their credibility as writers. (Standards 5.4, 5.5)

The following example of a factual story might be helpful:

> *This morning I woke up to the sound of my alarm clock. I fed my cat and made breakfast for myself. Then I showered. I got dressed and brushed my teeth. I said goodbye to my family and got in my car. It was raining, so I drove carefully. I got to school and came to the classroom to get ready for the day.*

The same story told with opinionated language might sound like the following:

> *Waking to the annoying sound of my alarm clock was the worst way to start my day. I had to feed my meowing cat right away or he would follow me around all morning. I started to make breakfast for myself, but I was rushing and accidentally burned the toast. I rushed out the door and almost forgot my keys. It was raining, and I was so upset because I hate the rain. Every other car was driving like crazy. I arrived at school and rushed to class before the bell rang. It was a hectic morning.*

Monitor Comprehension— Author's Point of View

Strategy 5: Biased Viewpoints in the News

Students need to be able to separate objective reporting from biased writing. Biased writing occurs when the author or the publication has a particular slant or prejudice that affects the way in which news is reported. A conservative newspaper and a liberal newspaper will report about the same event in very different ways. To determine bias in a piece of writing, students must be able to make inferences from the language of the author. They must be able to get beneath the literal meaning, or the surface meaning, of the author's words in order to determine the author's deeper meaning and influence.

Use the Biased Viewpoints in the News activity (page 51) to initiate a discussion on bias with students. In the meantime, collect a variety of brief newspaper articles from a few different newspapers. Ask around; you may find people who get out-of-town newspapers as well. If possible, try to find articles about the same topic. Use them with your students and conduct exercises similar to the one found on page 52. (Standards 5.5, 7.6)

Strategy 6: Writing with Bias

Students can also learn about bias by writing their own articles. Give students a set of facts such as the following:

- A developer wants to build houses on a bluff overlooking the ocean.
- The city council wants to limit the number of houses being built.
- The bluff is currently used for recreation by hikers and mountain bikers.

Have students pick the persona of one of the following reporters:

- A reporter for a local weekly newspaper that serves only people living around the bluff.
- A reporter for a big daily newspaper that supports local business.
- A reporter for a small daily newspaper that is pro-environment.

Allow time for sharing and discussing their reports. Have students listen for and identify evidence of bias in each other's work. Use the Objectivity in the News activity on page 53. (Standards 5.5, 7.6)

Monitor Comprehension—Author's Point of View

Strategy 7: Persuasive Points of View—Editorials

Opinion and bias, both intentional and unintentional, are two means by which authors express their points of view. Sometimes, however, authors have a straightforward task, which is to persuade the reader to adopt the same viewpoint as their own. Authors give the reader good reasons to change his or her mind about a subject or event. Editorials accomplish this task. A well-written editorial gives the opinion of the author and also attempts to persuade the reader to adopt his or her point of view. Expose students to a variety of editorials. Point out their relationship to current events, the author's opinion, and the persuasive language that the author uses to sway the reader. You may use the exercise on page 54 to initiate your discussion. (Standards 5.5, 7.6)

Strategy 8: Evaluating the Author's Word Choice

An author's word choice can greatly affect whether a piece of writing is controlled and objective or highly emotional and biased. Have students read example texts to practice identifying the kinds of language authors use in their writing. Students can use a plus sign (+) to indicate the use of precise, controlled language and a minus sign (–) to indicate the use of emotional, biased language. Use the Evaluating the Author's Word Choice activity (page 55) for practice with this strategy. (Standards 5.5, 7.6)

Strategy 9: Compare and Contrast

Collect news articles and editorials on the same subject matter or event. Have students compare and contrast the author's viewpoint (e.g., subjective vs. objective, neutral vs. biased, etc.). Also have them jot down the factual information found in each type of writing. Discuss the language that the authors used. Ask students about the emotional content of each type of writing. Which used more adverbs and adjectives? Did one piece use metaphors or other imagery to make a point to the reader? Is there evidence of bias in the supposedly neutral article?

You may have students use a Venn diagram to help them organize their thinking. Either as a class or individually, have them list facts included in both types of writing within the intersection and the other content in the remaining parts of the circles. (Standards 5.5, 7.5)

Strategy 10: Letters to the Editor

Letters to the editor are a vital part of any newspaper. In such letters readers can point out what they believe to be an author's bias, make an argument against an editorial writer, or make a point that an author may have missed. Pick a controversial newspaper editorial or article for students to read; then follow the letters to the editor that respond to it. Study the editorial and rebuttal letters to determine the author's point of view. How does each writer use the facts to support his or her argument? What emotional language does each writer use to sway the reader? As an extension, encourage students to write their own letters to the editor, either individually or as a class. (Standards 5.5, 7.4)

Monitor Comprehension—
Author's Point of View

Strategy 11: Propaganda Techniques

Secondary-level students have been exposed to thousands of commercials and advertisements through television, radio, magazines, and even the Internet. Teaching them to recognize the different techniques used by the media and advertisers to get the public to buy their products and services will help them become critical readers.

Begin by explaining the eight common propaganda techniques:

Testimonial—Persuasive statements made by people (often celebrities or sports stars) who claim to have personal experience with the product. For example, a basketball star selling soap claims it cleans better than other soaps, even though he is not an expert on soap.

Bandwagon—These statements attempt to make the reader believe that everyone is buying the product. For example, "Everyone loves our new breakfast cereal. Try Granny's Brannies."

Name-calling—These statements claim that one product is better than another. They represent other products, services, or ideas negatively. "Cleano is not gritty like Scrub-Away."

Facts Left Out—Statements leave out facts that may influence the reader not to buy the product. For example, cigarette ads have the Surgeon General's warning about the dangers of smoking in very small print at the bottom of the ad.

Opinions as Facts—These statements present opinions as factual information. "This watch is the most accurate timekeeper. It is the most attractive one I've seen."

Use of Numbers and Statistics—The author uses statistics to give the subject greater importance. "Nine out of 10 hospitals give this pain medicine to their patients."

Quotation out of Context—The writer quotes a source without giving the entire quotation. "This book should be on everyone's list. . . ." Left out was the rest of the quote: "to keep out of the hands of children because it has too much violence and too many racist characters."

Red Herring—These statements are intended to mislead the reader. "Wash-O laundry detergent makes your clothes smell fresh and clean." This ad doesn't say it cleans the clothes.

Students can bring in examples of each technique, or you can provide them with appropriate magazines and newspapers you have collected for use in the classroom. Students can work in pairs or groups to create a poster with one example of each technique or a poster collage with many examples of one specific propaganda technique. Groups or partners can explain their posters to the class, or they can read examples from their posters and have the class identify which technique the poster illustrates. Display the posters around the classroom. The Propaganda Techniques activity (page 56) gives students practice in identifying each propaganda technique. (Standards 5.1, 5.5)

Monitor Comprehension—
Author's Point of View

Strategy 12: Personal Points of View—Essays, Memoirs, and Autobiographies

Essays, memoirs, and autobiographies represent a special form of nonfiction. A single truth—the author's—forms the basis for these types of writing. For this reason, they are generally the strongest expression of a nonfiction writer's point of view. These texts contain more voice, reflecting the writer's personal expression through choice of language and attention to detail. Though more personal, essays, memoirs, and autobiographies may still carry a theme or attempt to persuade the reader to a particular point of view. Use the following examples to discuss with students the points of view or voice that can be found in these types of writing.

ironic	sarcastic	mournful
shameless	heroic	stodgy
dramatic	self-pitying	adamant
funny	angry	

You can see that it can be quite challenging to come up with just the right adjectives to describe an author's point of view. Gather examples of essays and such to share with students. Have them discuss the "truth" of what the author is stating. Discuss the fictional devices that the nonfiction writer might employ in order to strengthen his or her voice (e.g., metaphor, irony, and personification). See pages 57 and 58 for practice. (Standards 5.1, 5.5)

Monitor Comprehension— Author's Point of View

Fact vs. Opinion Partner Chart

Directions: With your partner, read the assigned text to find as many facts as you can on your topic. Write facts from the text in the left column. Each partner writes an opinion in his or her column for each fact.

Facts from text	Opinions of partner 1	Opinions of partner 2

Monitor Comprehension—Author's Point of View

Fact vs. Opinion—Separating Fact from Opinion

Directions: Many types of nonfiction writing contain opinions as well as facts. Opinions are statements that can be debated because they are based on information that cannot be proven. Facts are statements that can be proven and are not easily argued. To change a factual statement, there may even need to be experimentation or investigation. Read the statements below and determine which is an opinion and which is a fact.

Peppermint makes a refreshing iced tea.

Peppermint can be used to help settle an upset stomach.

The first statement contains an opinion. The statement can be debated because people who dislike peppermint would not find a tea made from it refreshing. The second statement is a fact. Mint has been used in many cultures to help ease the stomach. Also, the second statement uses conditional language. It says that peppermint can be used; it does not say peppermint must be used.

Often, opinions make generalizations, while facts are very specific. Read the statements below and determine which is broad and which is specific.

For many young people, listening to loud music helps them release tension.

Everyone loves to relax by dancing and listening to music.

The second statement, an opinion, is broad. Look at the language of the sentence. The word *everyone* means just that. Is this statement true? Does everyone love to relax by listening to music? The first statement, a fact, is specific. It contains specific adjectives—many, young, loud. If you investigated the statement, you would most likely find that it is true, or very nearly so.

Directions: Read the statements below. Place an **O** on the lines next to the statements that are opinions and an **F** on the lines next to the sentences that are facts.

_____ 1.   No one likes to go to the beach when it is cold.

_____ 2.   Many people save money at the market by clipping coupons.

_____ 3.   Cats are always annoying.

_____ 4.   Green is a restful color for a bedroom.

_____ 5.   Hummingbirds move very quickly as they travel from flower to flower.

_____ 6.   The best way to cook a potato is by boiling.

_____ 7.   To keep gardens free of weeds, use plenty of mulch such as wood chips.

_____ 8.   All toddlers love to chew on plain bagels.

_____ 9.   Many people give one another flowers on Valentine's Day.

_____ 10. The best cake for a party is chocolate.

Monitor Comprehension— Author's Point of View

Point of View

Like fiction, nonfiction can be written from three different points of view. Which one is used will depend on the type of writing and the author's purpose.

First-person point of view

- "I" is the narrator
- Subjective writing that includes opinions and feelings
- Eyewitness accounts, editorials, autobiographies, essays, reviews
- Example: I will remember the Northridge earthquake.

Second-person point of view

- Refers to "you" in the narrative
- Writing that the author wants the reader to identify with
- Advertising, propaganda, campaign messages
- Example: Your vote is needed to put a stop to ocean pollution.

Third-person point of view

- Objective writing that omits opinions and feelings
- News items, in-depth articles, reports, research, history and science texts, how-to manuals
- Example: To assemble, insert Tab A in Slot B and give one-quarter turn.

Directions: Complete the following activities:

1. Rewrite the following in third-person point of view as if you were writing a subjective report. Share your paragraph with classmates.

   As the flood waters rose, I began to grab belongings and haul them out to the car. I heard a tree branch snap in the wind, then fall to the ground with a thunderous crunch. My neighbor's windshield was demolished! I jumped into my own car and sped away. Water completely covered the bridge. I turned around, knowing my only hope was to go farther inland where hopefully the rain hadn't fallen so hard.

2. Select a paragraph from a news article and rewrite it in first-person point of view. Be creative and add interesting details such as your own thoughts and feelings. Share your paragraph with classmates.

3. Write an advertisement for a popular soft drink in second-person point of view. Try to get your reader motivated to buy the product by using language and examples that will help them identify with the product. Share your ad with your classmates.

Monitor Comprehension— Author's Point of View

Biased Viewpoints in the News

Reporters who write objectively give the reader facts rather than opinions. However, most newspapers have a bias, or viewpoint, that may cause news to be reported in a way that goes beyond fact. Unless you are familiar with the bias of a newspaper, you may not understand that the reporter is trying to change the way you think about events.

Directions: Read the articles and the annotations (notes) below and think about the bias of the author.

Article 1

The consumer won yet another battle against big tobacco companies. Monday, Tom Smith of Wheezeburg, Virginia, won a lawsuit against the Green Leaf Tobacco Co., for whom Mr. Smith worked for many years. Smith claimed that the Green Leaf poisoned its workers by giving them free cigarettes. Smith suffers from lung cancer and he has not been able to quit his smoking habit. He blames his smoking habit on his employer. A spokesman for the Green Leaf Tobacco Co. says that they will appeal the decision.

Article 2

The Green Leaf Tobacco Co. will appeal the lawsuit won Monday by bitter ex-worker Tom Smith. Smith claimed that the free cigarettes given to him by Green Leaf caused his lung cancer. However, spokespeople for Green Leaf said that Smith did not have to take the free cigarettes. In fact, Smith continued to smoke even after he knew he had cancer. Smith appeared smug over the judge's decision, stating, "I knew justice would prevail."

- Notice the first sentence of each report tells you about the author's viewpoint. One article seems to cheer for Mr. Smith; the other for the tobacco company.

- Both articles objectively report that the tobacco company gave free cigarettes to Mr. Smith.

- While both articles report that Mr. Smith has lung cancer, one article infers (suggests) that Mr. Smith got cancer because the company gave him cigarettes. The other article infers that Mr. Smith caused his own cancer by accepting the cigarettes from the company.

- The articles end in different ways, too. The first article objectively reports that the tobacco company will appeal the decision. The second article, on the other hand, makes a judgmental statement that Mr. Smith appeared smug, or pleased enough to be annoying to other people (especially, one might think, the reporter).

Clearly, one newspaper supports big business, while the other supports the consumer, or the common person on the street. Each newspaper is trying to influence the reader in some way. When you read a newspaper, you need to be aware of its bias so that you can pick out the facts and then form your own opinion.

Monitor Comprehension— Author's Point of View

Biased Viewpoints in the News *(cont.)*

Directions: Reread the articles on page 51 and complete the following activities:

1. Write down the facts of the articles as you understand them on the lines below.

   a. _____

   b. _____

   c. _____

   d. _____

   e. _____

2. Now write your opinion about the facts. Which side do you support? Why?

   _____

   _____

   _____

   _____

3. What headline or title do you think each author would write for his or her article? Write your idea for each headline on the lines below.

   _____

   _____

   _____

   _____

4. Rewrite the article so that it is objective (tells only the facts) on the lines below.

   _____

   _____

   _____

   _____

Extension: Read a newspaper article on your own. Write down the facts that you gather from the article. Then write your own opinion based on the facts. Is your opinion different from the author's?

Monitor Comprehension— Author's Point of View

Objectivity in the News

Directions: In general, news articles are supposed to be objective, omitting feelings and opinions. Instead, reporters rely on observations and quotes from people who participated in or witnessed the news event. Read the following news sentences and write an **O** next to the ones that are objective, and an **S** next to the ones that are subjective, or contain emotional language.

_____ 1. Bombs exploded over the desert today when Northern planes flew over the small island.

_____ 2. It was a terrible sight to see resident Tony Fick crying as he looked at the damage to his seaside home.

_____ 3. Temperatures are cooler than expected for this time of year due to an offshore pattern.

_____ 4. The courtroom audience held its breath as the judge read the guilty verdict to the court.

_____ 5. Once-quiet Crystal Creek will be disturbed today as bulldozers rumble through, clearing trees and brush for a new road.

_____ 6. Investigators are still trying to determine if the bees that stung two workers on Thursday were Africanized or domestic.

_____ 7. Teacher Alison Freehorn of Zenith School District was nominated as this year's teacher of the year.

_____ 8. There is nothing sadder than the aftermath of an automobile accident.

_____ 9. The construction of a much-needed soccer field was delayed once more as city council members wrestle each other over the question of budget.

_____ 10. The giant theater company, struck by hard times, is closing twenty of its megaplex theaters.

Extension: Find 3–5 newspaper articles and copy the lead sentences for each. Comment on whether the sentences are objective. Support your opinion by pointing out specific objective or subjective word choices.

Monitor Comprehension— Author's Point of View

Persuasive Points of View—Editorials

When an author's purpose is to change your mind, he or she uses persuasion. Persuasion means to influence someone by providing support for a specific viewpoint. Persuasion is not the same as opinion. When an author expresses an opinion, the purpose is not necessarily to persuade the reader, but to simply share a belief. A piece of persuasive writing, however, may be based on the author's opinion. Editorials are a type of persuasive writing found in newspapers. These are persuasive pieces of writing about current events, such as upcoming elections.

Directions: Read the annotated editorial below to see how the author used persuasion to influence the reader's thinking.

> *Western County does not need a new toll road. Two major freeways and three highways already serve its citizens. These roads are crowded at times, but even the Commissioner's own panel admits that only those drivers who can afford it will use the toll road. Therefore, the toll road will only slightly improve traffic for the rest of us, who will still be toughing it out on older roads that run through the less scenic parts of the city. For, as you know, the toll road will plow through pristine canyons. Sure, the designers have thought to put in tunnels beneath the road so that wildlife can pass from one side of the road to the other without risk of harm. I ask you, however, when was the last time you saw a deer hoofing it through a cement underpass? The luxury sedan drivers of our county should not benefit at the risk of losing our most beautiful resource—our beautiful canyons, our varied wildlife.*

- The author begins with a straightforward opinion.

- The author gives support to the opinion with facts: mainly drivers who can afford tolls will drive on the toll road, and the toll road will affect wildlife.

- The word "plow" gives a visual image of the toll road as an aggressor on the canyons.

- The author asks the reader to question the toll road design by providing a difficult-to-imagine scene.

- The author makes an observation about social class by suggesting that the county's wildlife belongs to everyone and should not be used to help the wealthy get to where they need to go faster.

Extension: Find a controversial article in the newspaper about which you have a strong opinion. Think about the most important facts in the article and use them in an argument that will persuade the reader to think as you think. Share your editorial with your classmates.

Monitor Comprehension—Author's Point of View

Evaluating the Author's Word Choice

Part I Directions: Read the examples of text below and identify whether the examples are specific and controlled or biased and overly emotional. Use a plus sign to identify precise, controlled language and a minus sign to identify biased, highly emotional language.

1. During the Civil War, the North and the South fought valiantly, but in the end the North triumphed and the slaves were freed.

   Plus (+) or minus (–) sign: _____

2. The Civil War was stupid! I agree that slavery was wrong, but there must have been a smarter way to end slavery. I think it is tragic that so many lives were lost because the opposing sides were too pigheaded to figure out a solution.

   Plus (+) or minus (–) sign: _____

Part II Directions: Reread the text examples and record specific sentences that illustrate the author's word choice in the left column. Then use a plus sign to indicate precise word choice or a minus sign to indicate biased or overly emotional word choice in the right column.

Examples from the text of the author's word choice	Evaluation of the author's word choice

Monitor Comprehension— Author's Point of View

Avoiding Bias in Storytelling

Directions: Read the propaganda techniques listed in Part I. Label each of the sentences in Part II with the correct propaganda technique.

Part I

➤ **Testimonial**—Persuasive statements made by people who claim to have personal experience with the issue

➤ **Bandwagon**—Statements intended to make the reader believe that "everyone is doing or believing" what the author is writing about

➤ **Name-calling**—Represents any alternative viewpoints negatively

➤ **Facts left out**—Leaves out facts that may influence the reader toward the author's viewpoint

➤ **Opinions as facts**—Represents the opinions of the author as factual information

➤ **Use of numbers and statistics**—Uses numbers to give the subject greater importance

➤ **Quotation out of context**—Quotes the source of information without providing all the information

➤ **Red herring**—Information intended to mislead the reader

Part II

Sentence or Scenario	Propaganda Technique
"Ninety-seven percent of all doctors agree that this toothpaste is truly the best for preventing cavities. Ninety-nine percent of customers agree."	
"The necklace is the most beautiful one I've ever seen. It is exquisite and represents the utmost in elegance."	
"Everyone agrees that our vaporizer is the best for helping kids recover from colds. Moms everywhere are buying this vaporizer. Please join moms from around the country and purchase our vaporizer."	
"This hair color product will give you vibrant, luxurious hair." (The advertisement left out the fact that the hair color product causes 5% of women to lose their hair.)	
"The characters in the movie are one-of-a-kind." The following information was omitted from the quotation: "They were rude, fake, and unbelievable!"	
"I can attest to the quality of this product. I have used it for the past 30 years and LOVE it!"	
"This dish detergent will leave your hands soft and smooth." (This ad misled the reader because it failed to mention whether the detergent actually cleans dishes!)	

Monitor Comprehension—Author's Point of View

Personal Points of View—Evaluating Author's Voice

Directions: Use the following graphic organizer to analyze the author's voice.

Remember: Voice is the way the author talks about a subject that reveals his or her personality as well as beliefs or feelings about the subject. Words that describe the author's voice in text include: excited, enthusiastic, cynical, skeptical, judgmental, angry, concerned, frustrated, positive, and negative.

Topic: _____

Intended audience: _____

Author's purpose: _____

_____

Words to describe the author's voice	Support from text

Monitor Comprehension— Author's Point of View

Personal Points of View—The Essay

Essays are very personal pieces of nonfiction writing. Essays can be about something unusual that happened to the author, or they can be about an everyday occurrence that the author sees in an unusual way. The personal tone of an essay invites the reader to get to know the author and to share in their perspective. Essays are read for pleasure rather than information.

Directions: Read the following essay and complete the activities below.

Simple pleasures are slowly disappearing from American life. Taking a stroll down a shady lane, feeding ducks a package of day-old bread, and looking for animals in the clouds have been replaced by television, movies, and video and computer games. Ask any child whether he or she would rather roll down a muddy hill or guide a hiccuping pink dinosaur on a skateboard through a maze and you know what the answer will be. The video game will win out, and the chance for a little getting-to-know-you conversation will be lost.

Decades ago, a movie was a treat, as was a chance to play a game of pinball. Nowadays, easy entertainment is everywhere. Why make an effort when, at the click of the button, a child can escape into a world more colorful than most adults can provide? It may come as no surprise, then, that I recently had to beg my daughter to join me on a walk in a sunny canyon overlooking the ocean. At first she dragged her feet, sad to be torn away from yet another movie about a loser team coming out as winners. But soon little lizards shot around this way and that, and rabbits, too. A coyote stumbled up onto the path. A hawk wheeled overhead. Wild flowers bloomed everywhere.

Soon we were talking about life, the universe, and everything. And at the end of the walk, my daughter said, "You know what, Mom? That was really fun." Telling her friends about an encounter with a real coyote beat watching a cartoon about one any day. A simple pleasure, to be sure, but unlike the hiccuping dinosaur, the coyote, with its black-tipped ears and delicate snout, would never be forgotten.

Activities

1. What is the author's point of view in this essay? (First person, second person, etc.) Why is it written in this point of view?

2. With what parts of the essay, if any, do you identify as a reader?

3. What is the message, or the author's "truth," contained in the essay?

Extension: Write your own essay about something you used to do regularly that you don't do anymore. Think about the tone of your essay. Are you happy or unhappy that the task or ritual is in the past? How can you let the reader know how you feel?

Passport to Comprehension

Activate and Connect

#50470 Successful Strategies

Activate and Connect

Introduction

Prior knowledge is everything that students have already learned. Students have prior knowledge about a topic, social experiences related to the topic, text structure, and reading strategies. Some students may have very limited prior knowledge in one or all areas; other students may have some knowledge, while still others may have quite a bit of knowledge. In the classroom, it is important to recognize the range of knowledge and experiences that students have and to provide them with a multitude of strategies that allow them to make connections between existing knowledge and new knowledge.

Connecting to Life Experiences

Students must become proficient at tapping into their deeply held cognitive structures called "schemata." Schemata (schema is singular) are the concepts that we develop about people, places, experiences, and events. For example, a small child knows the name of only one four-legged animal—"dog." Until he or she has more exposure and cognitive capacity, every four-legged animal is a dog. As the child acquires knowledge, the schema of four-legged animals expands to include cats, squirrels, and rabbits. In other words, the child assimilates or adds to the schema of four-legged animals. The child also accommodates or makes changes in previously held knowledge, that is, that there are four-legged animals other than dogs. Review with students what they already know about a topic and where they learned the information. Tapping into their life experiences is also highly motivating. After introducing a topic, here are some questions that may help students connect with their personal experiences:

- What memories do you have that connect with this topic?

- Have you ever seen a TV show or film about the topic?

- What feelings do you have in connection with the topic?

- Have you ever known someone who has told you about the topic? What was the person like?

- What concerns or interests you about the topic?

Asking Questions and Assessing Prior Knowledge

Questioning is a highly effective way to tap into prior knowledge. Questioning helps readers connect new knowledge with their existing understanding of a topic. Some sample questions include:

- What do you already know about _____?

- When you hear the word(s) _____, what do you think of?

- What events or ideas do you know that connect to the topic?

Activate and Connect

Asking Questions and Assessing Prior Knowledge *(cont.)*

Other techniques can also assess prior knowledge. The following are based on suggestions from Holmes and Roser (1987):

- **Free recall:** Have students tell anything that comes to mind about a topic.

- **Word association:** Ask students what comes to mind when you provide a few key words and phrases from the text.

- **Recognition:** Select key words and phrases associated with a text and display them along with erroneous words and phrases. Ask students which words and phrases are associated with the text based upon its title.

- **Structured questions:** Preview the text and prepare a set of questions designed to assess knowledge.

- **Unstructured discussion:** Ask students what they know about a topic, such as the expeditions of Lewis and Clark.

Evaluating Nonfiction Materials Using Prior Knowledge

Throughout their academic careers, students will need to locate and read a variety of nonfiction materials in order to access information necessary to complete their assignments. Students can use the following questions to help them evaluate nonfiction using their prior knowledge.

- Is this text organized in such a way that the information makes sense?

- How will the text features help me understand the topic?

- How does this text compare to another text on the same topic?

- What reading strategies will I need to use to make sense of the information?

Reformulating and Modifying Existing Knowledge

The purpose of learning new information is to build upon and clarify the existing information stored in a person's mind. Students must have many strategies to help them reformulate and modify their existing knowledge. Questions they can ask themselves include:

- How does this new information change what I know about the topic?

- How does this new information change what I believe about the topic?

- What new questions do I have?

Activate and Connect

Adjusting and Extending a Knowledge Base

While it is important that students tap into their prior knowledge, it is also important that they understand that as they learn new information, they will have the opportunity to adjust and extend their knowledge base. Often, we lead students to believe that they are simply to acquire and retain knowledge in order to pass a test or complete a unit of study. However, we must teach students that it is their responsibility to reflect on new knowledge, integrate it with their prior experiences, generate an expanded understanding of the information, and share their enriched understanding in meaningful ways. The activity on page 79 can help students extend their understanding.

Reflecting on New Learning

Reflecting on what has been learned is essential if students are to acquire and integrate new knowledge. Students need to have the ability to ask questions such as: How does this information confirm or contradict what I already know? How can I use this information in my life? What further questions do I have?

Formulating Ideas

After students engage in a variety of activities to tap into their prior knowledge, they need to be able to connect the text to their prior knowledge both during and after reading. Remind them to generate pictures in their minds, summarize, predict, and question as they read.

Applications to Real-Life Situations

Prior knowledge and personal experiences help us make sense of text information, but new text information feeds back into our real lives. Students need to understand that their new learning becomes the groundwork for future prior knowledge about a topic. Emphasize to students that they will need to apply what they learn in school to real-life situations and that building strong metacognitive processes will help them make learning meaningful.

Generating an Opinion

Students must become adept at using their prior knowledge about a topic to generate their own opinions. By teaching students to think about what they personally believe about the topic, teachers give them a built-in purpose for reading whenever they encounter new text. Encourage students to challenge their beliefs about the topic, the author's beliefs, their teacher's beliefs, and their fellow classmates' beliefs.

Activate and Connect

Constructing a Personal Response

When students can construct a personal response to text, they become more proficient at integrating new information. Reassure them that it is natural for them to ask questions as they read, such as: How does this information relate to me? How do I feel about this information? How can I use this information in my life?

Strategy 1: Text Walking and Picture Talking

Text walking (Harvey and Goudvis 2000) is a simple strategy in which the teacher leads students through a preview of the text using the metaphor of "walking and talking." Model how to preview the text by starting at the beginning of the text and talking about each text feature as you encounter it and how it helps you understand the major topics of the text. (Standards 5.6, 7.4)

Modeling this strategy with a book about the water cycle might sound like the following:

> **Teacher:** *I am going to "walk and talk" my way through this book about the water cycle. In that way I can get a sense of what this book is about and what the different text features will tell me about the topic. First, I see a heading called "Introduction." I think that I might be introduced to the concept of the water cycle and learn some general information about it. As I "walk" farther through this book, I see an illustration with captions. It looks as if it is explaining the stages of the water cycle. The captions use words such as "evaporation," "condensation," and "precipitation." I'm not sure what all those words mean, but I'm sure I will learn some new definitions when I reread the book. There are also some photographs of rain clouds that give more information about the water cycle.*

Strategy 2: Previewing and Self-Questioning

Present students with the Previewing and Self-Questioning activity (page 69) that will guide them through the previewing and self-questioning process. Begin by telling them the topic they will be exploring. You may want to show them a picture, colored overhead, or video clip to build interest. Then have students respond to the first question on the right side of the activity. Have them use the questions on the left side of the activity to preview the text in order to gather as much information as possible, using the text features for guidance. As they read, have them complete the remainder of the right side of the activity, making connections to their prior knowledge and thinking of ways to remember the information. (Standards 7.4, 8.2)

Activate and Connect

Strategy 3: KWL and KWL Plus

A highly effective strategy, KWL structures students' thinking before and after reading. Often it is difficult to begin this activity without building some background knowledge. As a class, complete the "knowledge" portion of the KWL chart (page 70). Then work with students to generate questions they have about the topic and complete the center column of the chart. You may want to use this chart as a previewing activity and have students ask questions based on the headings, subheadings, and pictures in the text. Next, have students read the text. When they are finished, they record what they learned and any new questions they may have. As an extension, use the KWL Plus question at the bottom of the activity to have students reflect on the importance of the information and how they will use or apply what they have learned to their lives. (Standards 5.6, 7.4)

Here is a completed KWL chart about the seasons:

What I Know	What I Want to Learn	What I Learned
There are four seasons in the year. Our weather changes with each season. Fall, winter, spring, and summer are all seasons.	What causes seasons? Do all regions have four seasons?	The different seasons are caused by the changing position of the earth in relation to the sun. Some regions only have two seasons, such as a wet season and a dry season.

Strategy 4: Anticipation Guides

Anticipation guides are used to stimulate thinking about a topic before reading a text. An anticipation guide contains a series of statements pertaining to a topic in a piece of text students are going to read. Before reading, students determine whether the statements are true or false or whether they agree or disagree with them. As they read the assigned text, they can focus on finding information in the text that supports or challenges their positions. When they complete the text, they can return to the anticipation guide to see if their opinions changed or stayed the same. They can also be required to point to places in the text that caused them to maintain or change their positions. (Standards 5.4, 7.4)

Activate and Connect

Strategy 4: Anticipation Guides *(cont.)*

Here is an example of an anticipation guide:

Topic: Abolition of Slavery

Before reading the text, read each statement and circle **A** if you agree or **D** if you disagree on the left. After you read the text, circle **A** if you agree or **D** if you disagree on the right.

Before		After
A D	1. There were slaves involved in the abolition movement.	A D
A D	2. Only Northerners thought slavery should be abolished.	A D
A D	3. Before Abraham Lincoln became president, little was done to end slavery.	A D

The anticipation guide takes time to construct, but any guides you create can be filed away for future use. The basic steps to constructing a guide are as follows:

1. Preview the text to determine the important concepts that you want students to think about.

2. Write short statements about those ideas. You only need to write five to 10 statements that are designed to activate prior knowledge and stimulate thinking. The statements do not need to be true or false statements as some of them will be based on the student's or the author's opinion.

3. Present the statements in the order in which the ideas appear in the text. (You can have students copy them into the center column of the guide, or you can type them into the column and make copies for the class.)

4. Distribute the guide. Allow time for students to complete the first part. Discuss their answers, directing them to support their positions.

5. Direct students to evaluate their opinions while they read the text. Then have them complete the second part of the guide.

6. Have a post-reading follow-up discussion concerning each statement. Have any of their opinions changed as a result of reading the text? Why?

An extended anticipation guide is a variation that requires students to write about whether the text supports their opinions. Students can either quote or paraphrase the text and refer to the page number. Permit students to disagree with an author's opinion if they can successfully create an argument that they can support with details. Anticipation guide templates are provided on pages 71 and 72.

Activate and Connect

Strategy 5: Structured Preview

While some students benefit from an informal preview of text, others need a more structured approach. Use the Structured Preview activity (page 73) to lead students through the text, making note of text structure, text features, key concepts/facts, predictions, and connections to prior knowledge. A structured approach will help struggling readers tap into their prior knowledge of both reading and life experiences related to the text. (Standards 5.4, 7.5)

Strategy 6: Riveting Reflections

Have students tap into their prior knowledge by using the activity titled Riveting Reflections (page 74). Continue by having students record what they learned after they read. Instruct them to reflect on their learning by identifying personal connections, evaluating the author, and generating questions. (Standards 5.6, 7.5)

Strategy 7: Predicting and Confirming Guide

Begin by having students preview the text and make predictions about the contents. Model how to create prediction statements and record them on the Predicting and Confirming Guide activity (page 75). Then have students read the text with the intention of finding information that either confirms or contradicts their predictions. Students should circle "yes" or "no" in the center column of their activities. Finally, have them explain the information that confirmed or contradicted their predictions. They can include what surprised, confused, or disappointed them about the text information. For example, if they were previewing a text about holidays around the world, they might make predictions about the kinds of celebrations that occur on these days. They might assume that Boxing Day is related to the sport of boxing. Once they read the text, they will be able to write the new information that supported or disputed their predictions. (Standards 5.6, 7.5)

Strategy 8: Visual Reading Guide

The Visual Reading Guide (page 76) provides struggling readers with a framework for previewing the text features in the reading material. Have students record what they can learn from the various text features (headings, subheadings, graphs, charts, diagrams, illustrations, photographs, and captions) in the left column of the chart. Then have them connect this information with their prior knowledge. For example, in a reading selection on slavery, students may encounter a picture of Frederick Douglass. Many will record that they knew he was an African American writer who fought for the abolition of slavery. (Standards 5.4, 7.5)

Strategy 9: Creating a Prereading Plan

Judith Langer (1991) created this strategy to assess students' depth of understanding of a topic. Using the Create a Prereading Plan activity (page 77), have students identify words that are associated with the topic. Then have them explain how they know the words. Through discussion, students clarify and refine their connections and understandings. Also, ask them to summarize their prior knowledge and identify what they hope to learn from the reading. (Standards 5.3, 5.4)

Activate and Connect

Strategy 10: Synthesizing Opinions

Secondary-level students must have the ability to synthesize various viewpoints and generate their own opinions based on the information they have gathered. Have students complete the Synthesizing Opinions activity (page 78) to identify the viewpoints of the author, their teacher, another source, and another classmate. Then instruct them to evaluate each viewpoint in order to generate their own opinion on the topic. (Standards 5.6, 7.3)

Strategy 11: Extending What You Have Learned

Divide students into teams and give each team an identical list of terms and concepts to find. Have the teams quickly preview the text to find the terms or concepts and develop a definition or association based on the text. The first team to finish wins. For additional practice with this strategy, see the activity on page 79. (Standards 5.3, 7.4)

Strategy 12: Partnered Reading

Pair each student with a partner. Discuss the topic or concept to be studied and perhaps allow them to briefly preview the text. Then have the pairs use the Partnered Reading activity (page 80) to identify and discuss their prior knowledge of the topic. They can compare the amount they know, the depth of their knowledge, and their interest in the topic. After reading, instruct them to identify how the text connected to their prior knowledge and determine which partner found information that most strongly connected to prior knowledge. This discussion will help them learn and retain the new information. Model the process before they begin. (Standards 5.4, 5.6)

Below is a sample dialogue you and a student might model for the class:

Teacher: We are reading a book about geometry. I know a lot about geometry.

Student: I know a lot, too. I know that geometry is about shapes and lines.

Teacher: I can name many shapes. I'm going to write some of them on my activity.

Student: I've had many experiences with shapes since kindergarten, like toys that come in different shapes.

Teacher: I also know that geometry is about putting shapes together to make other shapes. I've seen that done with tangrams.

Student: I want to write the definitions of some shapes and mention how many sides and corners shapes have.

Teacher: That is good information. I will include other words associated with geometry, like parallel and angle, but I'm not sure of the definitions. Do you know the meanings?

Activate and Connect

Previewing and Self-Questioning

Directions: Preview the text before reading and complete the left column. Before and during reading, answer the questions in the right column.

Previewing (before reading)	Self-questioning (before and during reading)
What information seems to be significant and important?	What information do I already know about the topic?
Which text features seem important? (captions, charts, graphs, diagrams, maps, photographs, illustrations, headings, subheadings)	How does the information I am reading connect to what I already know?
	How will I remember this information?

Activate and Connect

KWL and KWL Plus

Directions: Complete the left and center columns before reading. After reading, complete the right column.

What do I already know?	What do I want to know?	What did I learn?
What I know: How I know:	Questions about the topic:	What I learned: What I still want to learn:

KWL Plus

Reflection: Why is it important for me to know this information? How can I use this information?

_____

_____

_____

_____

_____

Activate and Connect

Anticipation Guide (Agree/Disagree)

Directions: Record statements about the topic in the center of the chart. Before reading, decide whether you agree or disagree with each statement by placing a check in the appropriate box under the "Before Reading" heading. After reading, think about the information you read and whether it changed your opinion about any of the statements related to the topic. Then place a check in the appropriate box under the "After Reading" heading.

Before Reading *After Reading*

Agree	Disagree	Statements about the topic	Agree	Disagree

Activate and Connect

Anticipation Guide (True/False)

Directions: Record statements about the topic in the center of the chart. Before reading, decide whether the statements are true or false and place a check in the appropriate box under the "Before Reading" heading. After reading, think about the information you read and whether the statements are true or false. Then place a check in the appropriate box under the "After Reading" heading.

Before Reading | | | *After Reading* |

True	False	Statements about the topic	True	False

Activate and Connect

Structured Preview

Directions: Preview the text to determine these elements.

Topic: _____

Text structure (description, compare/contrast, cause/effect, listing, problem/solution): _____

_____

_____

Text features: _____

_____

_____

_____

Key concepts	Facts

Prediction about what I will learn: _____

_____

_____

_____

How will this information connect to what I already know? _____

_____

_____

_____

Activate and Connect

Riveting Reflections

Directions: Use the activity below to reflect on new information about the topic.

Before reading: What do you already know about the topic? What do you expect to learn?
After reading: What did you learn?

Personal reaction: How did this information make you feel?	**Critical reaction:** How could the author have done a better job?	**Questions:** What further information do you want to know?

Activate and Connect

Predicting and Confirming Guide

Directions: Make predictions about what you will learn before you begin reading. As you read, determine whether your predictions were confirmed. Then explain using text information.

Predictions about the content (What will I learn?)	Confirmed by the text	Explanation
	YES NO	
	YES NO	
	YES NO	
	YES NO	
	YES NO	
	YES NO	

Activate and Connect

Visual Reading Guide

Directions: Preview the text and record as many details as you can regarding the text features listed. Then identify what you already know about the information contained in these text features.

Visual cues or text features	What I already know
Headings:	
Subheadings:	
Boldfaced or italicized words:	
Illustrations, photographs, and captions:	
Charts, graphs, and diagrams:	

Creating a Prereading Plan

Directions: Complete the following activities to make a plan for reading.

Topic: _____

Make a list of words you associate with the topic:

_____

_____

_____

Choose three words from your brainstorming above and record them in the left column of the chart below. Then answer the question in the top right column of the chart.

Words	What made you think of this word in connection with the topic?

Write a brief summary of what you already know about the topic: _____

_____

_____

_____

_____

What new information do you hope to learn? _____

_____

_____

_____

_____

Activate and Connect

Synthesizing Opinions

Directions: Identify several different viewpoints about the topic in the article you read. Then complete the box at the bottom of the page by generating your own opinion about the topic.

What does the author believe about the topic?	What does my teacher believe about the topic?
What does one other source say about the topic?	What does my classmate believe about the topic?

What do I believe about the topic?

Activate and Connect

Extending What You Have Learned

Directions: Use the activity below to activate prior knowledge, reflect on what you have learned, and extend your understanding.

Activate your prior knowledge	Reflect on what you have learned
Before reading: What do you already know about this topic?	After reading: What did you learn and how does it fit with what you already know?

Create something new to show your understanding: Write a story, poem, diary entry, letter, or draw a picture.

Activate and Connect

Partnered Reading

Directions: Each partner takes turns recording prior knowledge and its connection to new knowledge. Then discuss the reflection question and record your response on the lines provided.

Topic: _____

Partner 1: Prior knowledge about the topic	**Partner 2:** Prior knowledge about the topic
Partner 1: How does the information you have learned connect to your prior knowledge?	**Partner 2:** How does the information you have learned connect to your prior knowledge?

Reflection: Which partner's prior knowledge was more closely connected to the text? Explain.

_____

_____

_____

_____

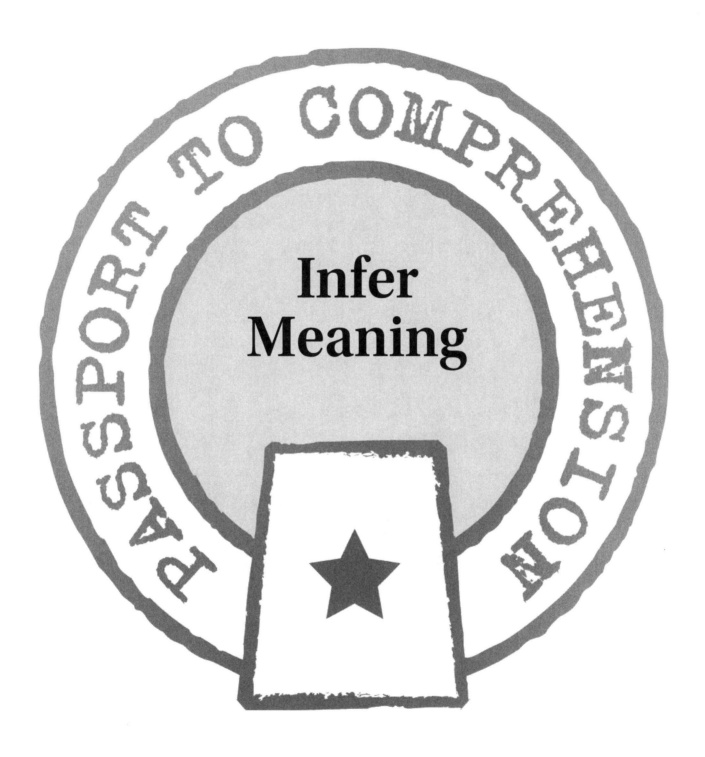

Infer Meaning

#50470 Successful Strategies

Infer Meaning

Introduction

To gain meaning from text, students must be able to infer. Inference is the process of judging, concluding, or reasoning based on given information. Strategies for inferring are closely related to those used for visualizing. While visualizing involves mental images, inferring has to do with words and thoughts; when used together, inferring and visualizing strengthen understanding.

The process of inferring involves reader interpretation of the text. A capable reader will work hard to discover the meaning of unclear words, terms, or concepts and connect them to the rest of the text. He or she will make defensible inferences that will explain the problems, places, or information in the text, using appropriate examples such as quotes, facts, evidence, and sources. In other words, a good reader will use good sources and/or quotes to support inferences and opinions. Perhaps most importantly, the capable reader will connect his or her inferences to the overall main idea or historical or cultural perspective.

Raising Questions

An effective method for increasing students' inferring skills is to ask many questions. Questions should be both **text explicit** and **text implicit**, but text-implicit questions are the ones that require inferential, divergent thinking.

Text-explicit questions are those questions where students can find the answer directly from the reading. No inference is required to arrive at an answer. Text-explicit comprehension requires the reader to read the lines and state what the author of the text says. There is typically only one correct answer to text-explicit questions.

On the other hand, **text-implicit** questions require the reader to combine what is read with other information based on prior knowledge and experience. The reader must read between the lines, and there are usually several plausible answers. Additionally, asking questions that require students to think on their own and to go beyond the text is the highest level of questioning.

Infer Meaning

Making Observations

Proficient readers make observations about text features, text content, and the author's choices. Insightful observations provide the groundwork for conclusions and inferences. For example, when a reader can identify specific aspects of a text feature, the likelihood of making critical inferences about the connection between the text feature and the author's purpose is greatly increased. Some ways to increase students' observational skills include teaching students how to:

- skim and scan for specific text features or content

- read silently and generate questions

- read with a partner and generate questions

- pause during reading to respond, react, and reflect

- reread for clarification

Making, Confirming, and Revising Predictions

Before students read, they must be able to make predictions about the information they are about to learn. To make predictions, they need to preview the text and infer what the author wants them to learn. Then, while students read, they need to think about their earlier predictions for the purpose of confirming or contradicting their initial thinking. As they continue reading and when they are finished reading, they need to revisit and revise their earlier predictions and examine how the author was shaping the information in order to influence the reader's final understanding of the text. Students need to be able to predict the overall meaning of the text and how they will use the information once they are finished reading. They need to be able to draw inferences and predict outcomes. For example, if students are reading about the court cases *Brown v. Board of Education* or *Plessy v. Ferguson,* they need to think how these cases connect to the concept of civil rights that they are studying. By drawing inferences about this connection to the civil rights movement, they will be able to predict what they will need to do with the information once they are finished reading.

Infer Meaning

Making Interpretations

When students make interpretations about text meaning, they are tapping into higher-order thinking skills. Questioning, visualizing, and inferring are developmental processes that aid readers in deepening their interpretations of the text. Proficient readers will examine cause-and-effect relationships, compare and contrast information, and engage in problem-solving techniques in order to gain more from the text than what is merely on the page. Some readers believe that nonfiction text simply contains information to be learned. It is important to communicate the significance of interpreting nonfiction text and to dispel the notion that the information is simply to be acquired. Students need to be able to evaluate the author's message, understand how their beliefs and attitudes about the topic are being shaped, and connect the text information with what they have already learned about the topic.

Conveying Underlying Meanings

It is important that students be able to identify and convey the underlying meaning in text. Often authors weave their bias throughout the text in such subtle ways that it is difficult for even the most astute reader to identify their intentions. The following questions will help students identify the underlying meaning in a text:

- What does the author believe about the topic? How do you know?

- What does the author want you to learn from this article?

Give students multiple opportunities to convey the meaning of a text to other students. Also provide them with opportunities to generate their own expository writing and evaluate it for underlying meaning. The Conveying Underlying Meanings activity (page 91) gives students practice in discovering meaning.

Making Speculations

Speculating about future events in the text, their implications for the reader, and the importance of text information helps readers build the foundation for drawing conclusions and making inferences. When students wonder about the text, they:

- create mental images in order to develop a clearer picture of the text

- link personal experience and prior knowledge to the text

- develop deeper levels of comprehension

- gain an increased appreciation for reading

Infer Meaning

Reacting

While proficient readers react to text in a variety of ways, struggling readers do not have a mental "tool box" to use to respond to text by inferring and drawing conclusions. Students need to be taught how to identify important text information, choose a method for reacting, and link prior knowledge and personal experience to the text.

Identifying and Assessing Evidence

An effective way to teach students to identify and assess evidence is to present them with a question that requires them to read in order to answer the question. Then require them to gather text evidence to support the answer to the question. Show them how to assess the validity of the information, the credibility of the sources, and the comprehensiveness of the information.

Using Strategies Independently

One of the best ways to develop student proficiency is to allow them to work in groups to practice strategies. Socialization and collaboration are highly motivating to students and are excellent vehicles for providing guided practice toward mastery. Some tips for supporting group work include:

- Provide step-by-step directions about what you expect from students.

- Assign roles and responsibilities to each group member.

- Require students to "publish" their work, either through oral sharing or a written assignment that will be posted in the classroom.

Once students have had exposure to group work, make sure to provide them with opportunities to use the skills that they have learned independently.

Strategy 1: Bloom's Taxonomy

When formulating questions from a particular text, focus on important aspects of the reading. Questions that are created to promote effective interactions with a text will help students avoid focusing on trivial facts and get right to the heart of the reading goals. Using question stems that move through Bloom's Taxonomy will take the students from text-explicit comprehension to text-implicit comprehension and will assist students in gaining a more meaningful understanding of the material. Teachers can use pages 89–90 as a reference for question-oriented activities.

Teachers will need to teach questioning skills in order for struggling readers to learn how to raise questions and find answers. Additionally, proficient readers will need guided practice to strengthen their existing questioning skills. When readers ask questions such as, "How does my prior knowledge help me understand the text?" and "How does using my visualization techniques help me create a complete picture of what's going on in the text?" their abilities to make inferences develop. (Standards 7.5, 8.2)

Infer Meaning

Strategy 2: Inferring about the Author

Begin by having students read the text and identify important events. Instruct them to use the Inferring about the Author—Part I activity (page 92) to record relevant text information. Have them use the right side of the double-entry journal to reflect on what the author wants them to learn, what the author believes about the subject, and whether they share the author's beliefs. The second part of the activity (page 93) can also help them infer the author's intent. (Standards 5.6, 7.5)

Strategy 3: Text on the Page/Text in My Head

One of the goals of sound reading instruction is for students to understand that the words on the page do not hold all of the meaning of the text. Have them use the activity (page 94) to record the specific information from the text on the left, and the "text in their heads" on the right side of the journal. Students must learn that the text in their heads is a compilation of all the prior knowledge and personal experiences that they bring to their reading experiences. (Standards 5.6, 7.5)

Strategy 4: Text Coding for Inferential Thinking

Providing students with a text-coding system can be a highly effective way for them to keep track of important text information that they would like to revisit. Have them use the Text Coding for Inferential Thinking activity (page 95) to record text information that corresponds with the coding that they used to mark the text itself or on a sticky note. Then have them write a detailed response or explanation that demonstrates their abilities to infer, predict, draw a conclusion, question, or make connections to prior knowledge. (Standards 5.6, 7.5)

Strategy 5: Making Conceptual Inferences

Using concept-based principles is the most effective way to help students retain factual information. Make sure to identify the concept that you want students to learn throughout the course of the unit. Present them with guiding questions that will help them categorize and make sense of the vast amounts of information they will be learning. Give them the Making Conceptual Inferences activity (page 96) and have them record facts from the text on the left and their inferences on the right. (Standards 5.6, 7.5)

Strategy 6: Making Global Inferences

Have students use the Making Global Inferences activity (page 97) to make inferences about people, events, settings, and other important facts in the text. Instruct students to make a connection to the concept being studied and the guiding questions they are investigating. Consider dividing students into groups of four and having each member take responsibility for one of the boxes on the inferences chart. (Standards 5.6, 7.5)

Infer Meaning

Strategy 7: Insightful Interpretations

Begin by providing students with a purpose for reading. You may want to remind them of the concept they are studying and refer them to guiding questions. Give students the Insightful Interpretations activity (page 98), and have them record significant text information and their own inferences about the text. Then have them discuss their observations with a partner and record their inferences. Give students an opportunity to read about the topic from another source and make an inference. Finally, share your inferential interpretation of the text. (Standards 7.4, 7.5)

Strategy 8: Partnered Reading

Provide students with sentence starters in order to guide them in the Partnered Reading activity (page 99). Give them an opportunity to read together and record significant text information and related inferences. Have students highlight and discuss the similarities and differences between their inferences. (Standards 7.4, 7.5)

Strategy 9: Perceptive Predictions

Have students read a persuasive piece of text. Instruct them to complete the Perceptive Predictions activity (page 100) and identify the issue, solution, and pros and cons of the topic presented in the article. Finally, have students identify the author's beliefs about the topic and what the author expects the reader to do with the information. (Standards 7.4, 7.5)

Strategy 10: Making Text-Feature Inferences

Before reading, review with students the concept being learned and the guiding questions. Preview the text by asking students about the text features and their possible connections to the topic and concept they are learning. As students are reading, have them record their observations about the text features using the Making Text-Feature Inferences activity (page 101). Then have them make inferences about the text features' connections to the major concept being studied. (Standards 7.2, 7.5)

Strategy 11: Making Artistic Inferences

Provide students with the Making Artistic Inferences activity (see page 102). Then have them draw an illustration of the concept or topic. You will find that students will combine the information from the text itself and the "text in their heads" to create their illustrations. Instruct students to reflect on their illustrations and make observations about the details, colors, and ideas derived from their prior knowledge about the topic. (Standards 5.4, 7.5)

Infer Meaning

Bloom's Taxonomy

Bloom's Taxonomy is a classification system that uses educational objectives for developing higher-level thinking skills. In order to meet the needs of a variety of learners, teachers can utilize this model to present ideas and concepts at many different levels. When writing your own questions, include at least one question from each level.

1. **Knowledge**

   Students recall, remember, memorize, or recognize information. This is the basic level that establishes a foundation for better understanding. Tasks include asking students to define, describe, label, locate, recite, select, memorize, recognize, name, state, identify, repeat, and list.

2. **Comprehension**

   This requires students to understand information and the focus is on the meaning and intent of the reading material. This level requires a translation of data from one form to another. When students are asked to restate, paraphrase, rewrite, convert, give examples, illustrate, summarize, explain, and locate, they are working at the comprehension level.

3. **Application**

   At this level, problem solving is required. Students use the information in the material to transfer their learning to new and concrete situations. Verbs to use in application questions include apply, modify, dramatize, translate, demonstrate, and construct.

4. **Analysis**

   Students examine specific parts of information to identify the underlying ideas. It is a strategy that is utilized when attacking a problem or reaching a decision. Tasks include asking students to analyze, classify, distinguish, subdivide, separate, differentiate, examine, calculate, compare, and contrast.

5. **Synthesis**

   Something fresh and different is done with the information; parts and elements of the material are put together in a new form. Verbs to use in synthesis questions include combine, compose, design, organize, invent, develop, plan, create, and devise.

6. **Evaluation**

   The highest level of the taxonomy, this requires assessment of the quality or judgment of the value of material based on internal evidence (logic) or external criteria or standards. Include words such as evaluate, recommend, summarize, debate, criticize, or judge.

Infer Meaning

Bloom's Taxonomy Question Stems

Consider students' levels of cognitive development according to Bloom's Taxonomy. Then use these stems to develop questions and prompts that will match their needs.

Knowledge

1. Who?
2. What?
3. When?
4. Where?
5. How?
6. List the facts in order.

Comprehension

1. What is meant by…?
2. Can you describe…?
3. What is the difference…?
4. What is the main idea…?
5. Why does…?
6. Explain why…

Application

1. Who would you choose…?
2. What would happen if…?
3. How would you…?
4. Do you know someone like…?
5. Would you do the same thing in the same situation?
6. If you had to…, what would you do?

Analysis

1. What part of the reading is the funniest?
2. What part is the most exciting?
3. What part is the saddest?
4. Which things are facts and which are opinions?

5. What can you do that is just like what the person in the story does?
6. List five compound words from the story.
7. What is the purpose of…?

Synthesis

1. Retell one event from an animal's point of view.
2. How could we/you…?
3. Make up another ending for the story that still fits the details.
4. Rewrite a sentence from the reading but change one thing in it.
5. Write a new title for this story.
6. Write a six-line rhyming poem about the reading.

Evaluation

1. Is the main character in this reading good or bad? Why?
2. Which is better…?
3. Would you agree that…?
4. What is your opinion of…?
5. Are they right to do…? Why or why not?
6. Compare two characters in the reading. Tell which one you think is better and why.

Infer Meaning

Conveying Underlying Meanings

Directions: Convey underlying meanings about the topic you read.

Underlying meaning: the author's hidden intent; information that you have to infer about the topic

Topic or concept: _____

Important text information	Key words, phrases, or concepts (context clues that help you infer the underlying meaning)	Underlying meaning

Infer Meaning

Inferring about the Author—Part 1

Directions: Record text information on the left side and inferences about the author on the right side.

Text information	Inferences
What is happening in the text? What events have occurred?	What does the author want me to learn from this? What does the author believe about the topic? Do I share the author's beliefs? Is the author making an impact on me?

Infer Meaning

Inferring about the Author—Part 2

Directions: Respond to the prompts and questions in order to draw a conclusion about the author's intent.

Title of text: _____

Main topic: _____

Important subtopics: _____

_____

_____

Text structure selected: _____

Text features included: _____

_____

Words or phrases that reveal the author's beliefs or opinions about the topic:

_____

_____

_____

Conclusion about the author's purpose (What does the author want the reader to gain from reading the information?):

_____

_____

_____

_____

_____

_____

_____

_____

Infer Meaning

Text on the Page/Text in My Head

Directions: Record significant information from the text on the left side of the double-entry journal. On the right side, record images, thoughts, and ideas from your own background knowledge that relate to the text, as well as inferences about the topic and text.

The text on the page	The text in my head

Infer Meaning

Text Coding for Inferential Thinking

Directions: As you read, use the codes below to mark in the margins or on a sticky note next to significant segments of text. Then use the chart to record the text information connected to the code in the left column of the chart and a response in the right column of the chart.

I = Inference   **?** = I wonder

P = Prediction   **PK** = Prior knowledge connection

C = Conclusion

Text information	Response or explanation (Remember that you are making an inference or prediction, drawing a conclusion, wondering about the text, or connecting to prior knowledge.)

Infer Meaning

Making Conceptual Inferences

Directions: Make inferences about the facts you are learning and their connection to the larger concept.

Concept being studied: _____

Guiding questions: _____

_____

Facts from the text	**Inferences** (How do these facts connect to the larger concept? How do these facts help me answer the guiding questions?)

Infer Meaning

Making Global Inferences

Directions: Make inferences about people, settings, events, and other related facts in the text.

Concept being studied: _____

Guiding questions: _____

_____

People in the text	Settings in the text
Inferences about connection to concept:	Text support or prior knowledge support:
Inferences about connection to concept:	Text support or prior knowledge support:
Events in the text	**Other related facts in the text**
Inferences about connection to concept:	Text support or prior knowledge support:
Inferences about connection to concept:	Text support or prior knowledge support:

Infer Meaning

Insightful Interpretations

Directions: Use this graphic organizer to read for significant information, make insightful interpretations, and gather additional interpretations from a partner and your teacher.

Text information	My interpretation

My partner's interpretations	My teacher's interpretations

Infer Meaning

Partnered Reading

Directions: In the top boxes, each partner should record significant text information. Then each should use the thinking stems below to make an inference about the text.

> This information connects to…
> I think that…
> I visualize…
> I predict…
> Perhaps the author wants us to think that…

Partner #1: Significant text information	Partner #2: Significant text information
Partner #1: Inference about the text	**Partner #2: Inference about the text**

Infer Meaning

Perceptive Predictions

Directions: Make a prediction about the text information.

Issue or problem:

Proposed solution:

Pros	Cons

Prediction: What are the author's beliefs about the topic? What does the author expect you to do with the information you have gained?

Infer Meaning

Making Text-Feature Inferences

Directions: Make inferences about the text features.

Concept being studied: _____

Guiding questions: _____

_____

Text feature (charts, graphs, diagrams, pictures, illustrations, captions, photographs)	**Inference about the text feature's connection to the major concept**

Infer Meaning

Making Artistic Inferences

Directions: Illustrate the inferences you make in your mind.

Words or phrases from the text that describe the topic or concept: _____

_____

_____

_____

Illustration of idea or concept

Look back at your illustration. What information (details, ideas, colors, etc.) did you include in the illustration that were not described in the text?

_____

_____

_____

Why did you add the information that you did to your illustration?

_____

_____

_____

Ask Questions

PASSPORT TO COMPREHENSION

Ask Questions

Introduction

What is the difference between active and passive readers? Active, skilled readers approach nonfiction text with questions such as "What is the meaning of the title?" "What type of text is this?" and "What does the author mean by this statement?" Finally, they think beyond the text by asking questions after they have finished reading, such as "Where can I find additional facts?" Their active questioning leads them to the next piece of text, the next piece of information. Through questioning, learning becomes an ongoing process.

Passive readers, on the other hand, may not realize that their comprehension will be improved by forming their own questions as they read. By not asking questions, passive readers miss making rich connections within the text and between their personal experiences and the text. Each reading assignment becomes a dead end rather than an invitation.

To turn passive readers into active ones, teachers need to model not only the process of questioning, but also an enthusiastic embrace of the process. Teachers must also model different types of questions. There are questions that require a simple factual answer, questions that require critical thinking, and even questions that perhaps will never be answered, such as "Why does every living thing eventually die?"

In addition to modeling, teachers must equip students with the skills to generate questions on their own. Some methods, such as brainstorming, are freewheeling ways for students to learn to actively form questions. Others, such as journalistic questions, give students a systematic method for creating useful questions.

Good questions engage a student's curiosity, encourage original thinking, assess a student's ability to recall and infer, and even prompt additional questions. Good questions excite and motivate reading. They propose and predict ideas. They help readers check for understanding. They beg for answers and are not easily brushed aside.

How is reading proficiency developed through reading? Questions are particularly motivating to secondary-level students because they are at a point in their lives where they want to understand and make sense of the world. When students are reading, questioning strategies can help arouse curiosity, provide direction for research, formulate a purpose for reading, and stimulate further reading and investigation about a topic.

In an educational climate driven by assessment and accountability, it is important to understand the difference between assessment questions and genuine learning questions. Typical assessment questions are those questions that we already know the answer to and that we use to measure the academic achievement of students. Genuine learning questions are those questions to which we do not know the answers, that arouse our curiosity, and that require further inquiry on the part of both the teacher and the student. There is a place in the classroom for both kinds of questions, and it is essential that students become proficient at using reading strategies that allow them to answer both kinds of questions accurately, elaborately, and confidently.

Ask Questions

Categorizing and Differentiating among Questions

When students are able to categorize the kinds of questions they are being asked, they are better able to understand their purpose for reading. Understanding and applying such strategies as the Question/Answer Relationships strategy can aid readers in knowing the kinds of reading and thinking they have to do in order to answer a question. In addition, question coding can help readers categorize a variety of different kinds of questions they will encounter across content areas. The skill of categorizing is one that is useful both in school and various real-world contexts.

Monitoring Comprehension

When teachers model reading strategies, it is important that they know how to gradually release the responsibility to students. Students must have access to a variety of strategies in order to clarify, revise, and reformulate their initial understandings of text content. There are two types of explicit modeling that can ensure that students move toward taking responsibility for monitoring their reading comprehension: talk alouds and think alouds (Roehler and Duffy 1991). In a talk aloud, the teacher presents students with the components of a monitoring strategy and then orally leads them through these steps by showing students how to apply the strategy. It is useful to make an overhead transparency of the steps of the strategy. For instance, when a graphic organizer is being introduced to the class, the teacher tells students the steps necessary to fill in the different parts of the organizer, but does not fill them in. Usually, in an introductory lesson, the teacher would show students the exact procedures needed to fill in the graphic organizer and do a sample in front of the class. The following is a partial example of a talk aloud for a web organizer:

> **Teacher:** I've written the steps that you should follow to fill in a web.
>
> **Step 1:** Read the selection to determine the main idea. Write it in the center oval.
>
> **Step 2:** Reread the selection. This time, stop as you identify details that support the main idea.
>
> **Step 3:** Write each supporting detail in the boxes surrounding the main idea.
>
> **Step 4:** Make sure all the boxes for supporting details are filled in.
>
> **Step 5:** Use the information on your web to write a summary of the selection you just read.

The teacher then takes students through the process necessary to do the steps but doesn't model aloud the thinking done to find the main idea or details, write the main idea or details, or write the summary. In Step 5 the teacher might say, "When you have finished your web, you will use all the information to write a summary of what you read." Then students apply the strategy to a text. Teachers use talk alouds to teach students how to use strategies.

Ask Questions

Monitoring Comprehension *(cont.)*

Think alouds require the teacher to explain the steps of the strategy and then share the actual thinking that accompanies the use of this strategy (Clark 1984; Meichenbaum 1985). Teachers should make their own confusion, misconceptions, general wonderings, and discoveries apparent. It is important to show students that an adult reader also has to wonder, clarify, and question in order to understand text information and that an adult can experience delight when finding the answer.

Organizing Content Knowledge

Students need to have a variety of techniques for acquiring content knowledge. In order to help them, teachers should consider focusing instruction on key concepts. The following are some basic questions that you can ask yourself when planning a unit:

1. What is the major concept being investigated or studied?

2. What are the guiding questions that will help students make sense of this topic?

3. What texts will I use to help students find answers to the guiding questions?

4. How will I help students organize the information that they find in order to maximize their content knowledge and its connections to the major concept?

The Reading Process

To become proficient readers, students must understand that reading is a process and that there are specific behaviors to engage in before, during, and after reading. Questioning skills must be developed at each stage of the reading process, and these questions can focus on either the content of the text or the process of reading. The following questions can be shared with students to guide their thinking before, during, and after reading:

Before Reading

- What do I already know about the topic?

- How do the title, headings, and subheadings reveal information about the topic?

- What strategies could help me make sense of the text?

During Reading

- What new information am I learning in order to clarify my original understanding of the topic?

- What strategies can I use to monitor my comprehension of the major themes and concepts?

After Reading

- What is my overall understanding of the topic?

- What strategy was most effective in helping me make sense of the information?

Ask Questions

Accessing Prior Knowledge

Students must access their prior knowledge in order to construct meaning. The following is a step-by-step process for connecting prior knowledge to the content learned during daily instruction. Post these questions on a chart or on the board to help guide students throughout their learning experiences in your classroom.

- What do I already know about the topic?

- How does the text connect to what I know?

- How does the connection further my understanding of the topic?

Making Inferences

Students will need to be adept at making inferences in order to make sense of complex text. Well-developed inferring skills allow students to connect their prior knowledge to the text and to comprehend the information at much deeper levels. The following are some questions that students can ask themselves to build inferring skills:

- How do I interpret this information?

- What are my observations after looking at headings, subheadings, and pictures?

- How does my prior knowledge help me make reasonable inferences?

Asking Questions to Seek Elaboration and Clarification

Students must be able to clarify and elaborate upon their initial understandings of text. In order to access deeper levels of meaning in the text, it is important for students to be able to ask themselves questions, such as:

- What is the information teaching me about the topic?

- What is the author's message?

- How do the details enrich my understanding of the main concept?

Ask Questions

Using Strategies Independently

The following strategies will help build students' proficiencies as readers. Adapt these strategies to suit the needs of your classroom. Remember the gradual release of responsibility. It is essential that students learn to use these strategies independently. This independence is achieved through teacher modeling, direct instruction, talk alouds, think alouds, and the expectation that students will internalize the modeling and apply the strategies to their own reading.

Strategy 1: Trivial Pursuit and Brain Quest

Divide students into teams and ask general questions from games such as Trivial Pursuit and Brain Quest. Give students a day to research various topics of interest and generate their own questions that can be used for cooperative games to answer knowledge-based questions. Gradually incorporate questions from concepts that students are learning in your classroom and require students to make inferences and extend their thinking. (Standards 7.5, 8.2)

Strategy 2: Partner Questioning

Students write five knowledge-based questions on a slip of paper using their class notes and information from the text. Pair each student with a partner, and have each partner ask a question while the other partner answers. This strategy helps students review material before a quiz, develop listening skills, and check for understanding during a lesson or unit. (Standards 7.4, 8.2)

Strategy 3: Question Web

The Question Web activity (page 115) is a great way for students to gather information about one question. These questions can be student- or teacher-generated. Students record their question in the center of the web. Then they read and research the answers to the question by accessing a variety of resources. It is particularly motivating to students if they can work as a team to gather the information to answer the question at the center of the web. After gathering enough information, they work together to synthesize what they have learned into a coherent response. Students will need you to model the synthesis of information. Write a sample question web on a large piece of butcher paper and then use two highlighters to code essential and extraneous information. Demonstrate how to blend, combine, and connect the essential information into a response to the question. (Standards 7.4, 8.2)

Strategy 4: Discussion Questions

Students often say they do not know what types of questions to ask when having a discussion about a text. Provide students with the list of discussion questions (page 116) to use to facilitate class or small-group discussions. Students can also use this list independently to guide their thinking while they read. (Standards 5.6, 8.2)

Ask Questions

Strategy 5: Question/Answer Relationships (QAR)

Teaching students to understand question/answer relationships can greatly aid their abilities to answer questions proficiently. QAR is a strategy for teaching students how to find answers to questions, especially those for which the answer may not be found in the actual text. Raphael (1982), who developed this technique, identified three types of questions:

Right-there questions: Questions for which answers are easily found in the text.

Think-and-search questions: Questions for which answers are embedded within the text in a way that makes them more difficult to find.

On-your-own questions: Questions for which the answers are not in the text. Students will need to think about the answer (On My Own) or go to another resource besides the text itself (Author and Me).

Example

This strategy used in social studies might elicit the following questions for the subject of Egyptian religion:

1. Right-there question: Who was the god of the living and the dead?

2. Think-and-search question: What beliefs did people have about Amon-Re?

3. On-my-own question: Why would religion be important to the people?

4. Author-and-me question: Why would Egyptians prepare so much for the afterlife?

This strategy used in math on the topic of an integer might look like the following:

1. Right-there question: What is an integer?

2. Think-and-search question: What types of integers are there?

3. On-my-own question: When would I use negative numbers?

4. Author-and-me question: How would I balance a checkbook?

Use the Question/Answer Relationships activity sheet (page 117) to guide students through the identification of questions. Then have students read a particular piece of text and use the appropriate code to apply their knowledge of QAR. (Standards 7.5, 8.2)

Ask Questions

Strategy 6: Stance Questioning

Stance questioning is a way to gain a picture of where the reader "stands" in relation to the text. When readers "enter" into a text, they begin to form a global understanding of the text. As they "move" through the text, they develop their interpretations and further their initial understandings. As they "exit" the text, they are able to relate personal experiences and prior knowledge to the text information. When readers have fully exited the text and gained some distance, they are able to analyze the author's decisions (based on the work of Judith Langer 1987). Stance questions can be divided into four categories:

Global Understanding—Being Out and Stepping Into the Text

Developing an Interpretation—Being In and Moving Through the Text

Reflecting on Personal Experiences—Being In and Stepping Out of the Text

Critical Response—Stepping Out and Analyzing the Reading Experience

Use the activity sheet on page 118 to allow students to choose questions within these categories to guide them as they move through the reading process. (Standards 5.4, 8.2)

Strategy 7: Double-Entry Journal

When students use double-entry journals, they are able to see the connection between the text and their thinking. Instruct students to divide their pieces of notebook paper in half and record text information on the left side and their reflections, questions, and/or responses on the right side. This strategic tool teaches students that they are not merely reading words and that their brains should be actively making note of both the text and the thinking that goes on in relation to the text. Have students read content-related text and use the Double-Entry Journal (page 119) to exercise their metacognitive skills. (Standards 5.6, 8.2)

Strategy 8: Digging Deeper

Students will begin by listing random, unconnected questions about a given topic. But as their reading and questioning skills improve, encourage them to build their questions so that each answer creates a deeper understanding of the topic or concept under investigation. Have students use the Digging Deeper chart (page 120) during or after reading to record significant text information and reflect on that text information by responding to the sentence starters on the right side of the chart. (Standards 5.4, 8.2)

Ask Questions

Strategy 9: Coding for Quality Questioning

Coding text is useful during reading to ensure that students are engaging with the information as they are reading. You can create codes simply by thinking of the topics, concepts, or ideas that you want students to reflect upon and then assigning a single letter to represent that idea. A particularly powerful set of codes includes the following: Text-to-Self (T-S), Text-to-Text (T-T), and Text-to-World (T-W). Readers will consciously make note of times when the text connects to their own lives, to another text, and to information related to the world. Students can write the codes directly on the text or on sticky notes. Use the reproducible on page 121 to have students use the codes to make more detailed reflections on the text. (Standards 5.6, 8.2)

Strategy 10: Text Questioning

Have students preview the text and generate as many questions as possible on the board. Then read the text aloud with students, pausing during reading to record more questions on the class list. After reading, record any final questions. Then go through the list and discuss the questions, placing a code of "T" next to any questions that were answered explicitly in the text. Discuss the remaining questions and how conceptual knowledge or inferences are needed to answer these questions. (Standards 5.4, 8.2)

Strategy 11: Concept and Fact Questions

Provide students with two sizes of sticky notes—large and small—to use when finding a concept or a fact. Instruct them to read the text information and record questions that require inferences, reference to concept knowledge, connections to other texts or prior knowledge, or further research on the large sticky notes. Essentially students are capturing the big ideas on the concept sticky notes. Instruct the students to record fact-based questions, right-there questions, and questions about vocabulary on the little sticky notes, intended to represent smaller ideas. After reading, create a T-chart on the board with "Concept Questions" on the left side and "Fact Questions" on the right side. Students place their sticky notes in the appropriate column. Discuss whether the questions are "correct" in that they do represent conceptual or factual information. Allow students to come to the board to choose a sticky note to which they will respond either orally or in writing. A template for a T-chart can be found on page 122 for students to use independently with other texts. (Standards 5.4, 8.2)

Ask Questions

Strategy 12: Question Squares

As students read, they should ask questions about what they are reading. Sometimes these questions can be asked of oneself, the author, the teacher, or other classmates. Using the Question Squares chart (page 123), students can record key information from their reading and then think of questions for these different audiences. (Standards 7.4, 8.2)

Strategy 13: Questions Before, During, and After

Using the Questions Before, During, and After chart (page 124), students can write the many questions they have before, during, and after reading. They can also record speculations and predictions. Having a chart to record this information provides some structure to help students guide their thinking. After reading, they can think of questions they still have and also record possible answers. This activity works well in small groups or pairs or with a student working independently. (Standards 7.4, 8.2)

Strategy 14: Questions on Trial

Use this strategy once students understand the importance of asking questions before, during, and after reading. Create a panel of four student judges who will analyze their classmates' questions. The panel must explain why a question is "good" or "better" based on the question's ability to enhance the knowledge of the questioner. There are no "bad" questions, only good questions and better questions. Assign weaker students to be judges only after they have seen several different panels of student judges. (Standards 7.4, 8.2)

Here is an example of one panel's assessment of classmates' questions:

Good question: When did Christopher Columbus discover America?

Panel's analysis: This is a good question, but it is very narrow. All you will learn from it is a date.

Better question: Why did Christopher Columbus set sail across the Atlantic Ocean?

Panel's analysis: This is a better question. It will lead you to a major understanding.

Good question: How was Christopher Columbus received by the natives he met?

Panel's analysis: This is a good question, especially if you give an explanation rather than a one-word answer.

Better question: What were the consequences of Christopher Columbus's discovery of America?

Panel's analysis: This is a better question because it will help you find out what happened in the long run.

Ask Questions

Strategy 15: Question Exchange

A question exchange lets students review information using their own questions. Each student prepares five thought-provoking questions and answers; these questions cannot have "yes" or "no" answers. Each student poses one of these questions to a classmate in round-robin fashion. The classmate gives an answer. If that answer is correct, then he or she asks a question of the next student. If the answer is wrong, then the one who asked the question asks the next student until a correct answer is given. It is best if students ask a question that has not already been asked; however, if necessary, they may repeat one. This strategy is good for review before a test because each student knows the answers to his or her original five questions plus the answers to all questions presented in class. The following is a sample of this strategy in action:

Alicia: (to Benito) "What territories did the U.S. acquire as a result of the Spanish-American War?"

Benito: "Puerto Rico, the Philippines, and Guam."

Alicia: "Right."

Benito: (to Christa) "When did the Spanish-American War begin and when did it end?"

Christa: "1861 to 1865."

Benito: "Sorry, that's wrong."

Benito: (to Dylan) "When did the Spanish-American War begin and when did it end?"

Dylan: "The Spanish-American War started and ended in 1898."

Benito: "Correct."

Strategy 16: "I Wonder... " Poems

After you have presented a topic or concept to students, have them work in groups to write an "I wonder… " poem. Instruct students to record all of their questions about the topic by starting with the sentence starter "I wonder… ." Post the poems around the classroom and have students refer to them while they learn the new topic or concept. Following is a sample of a poem with questions about bats:

> I wonder how a bat got its name.
> I wonder what bats like to eat.
> I wonder if bats are a kind of bird.
> I wonder where a bat lives.
> I wonder if bats are a friend or foe of humans.

Ask Questions

Question Web

Directions: Write your question in the center circle. As you read, listen, or do research, record your answers on the outer spokes of the web.

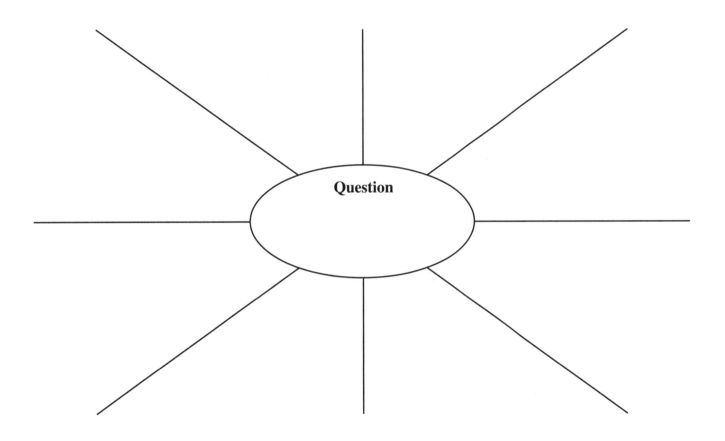

Synthesis of information: Use the most important text information to write a response to the question in the center of your web.

_____

_____

_____

_____

_____

_____

_____

Ask Questions

Discussion Questions

Questions for thinking about text content:

- What is the main idea of the text?
- What are the big ideas in the text?
- What is most interesting?
- What did you find confusing?
- Did you learn anything new?
- Did you learn anything that surprised or concerned you?

Questions for thinking about world connections:

- What do you already know about this topic?
- How does the text connect to topics or concepts you are learning in class?
- What new questions do you have about this topic?
- What current events connect to this topic?

Questions for thinking about a strategic approach:

- What parts of the text are difficult or confusing?
- What parts of the text are boring?
- What strategies can you use to make the text more interesting?
- What strategies can you use to better understand the text?
- Did your strategic attempts work? Explain.
- What new strategies can you use?
- Can you use part of a strategy you have learned to help you?
- Do you need to create a new strategy?
- What are your overall feelings about the text and how did you form these beliefs?

Questions for understanding the process of reading:

- What new information did you learn about reading?
- How can you apply your knowledge to reading other texts?
- Why is a strategic approach to reading important?
- What advice can you give to other readers about the process of reading?

Ask Questions

Question/Answer Relationships

Part A Directions: Read the following information aloud. Observe the differences among each of these four kinds of questions.

In the Text	In My Head
Right there: The answer to the question can be found easily and immediately in the text. The words used to create the question are the same words found in the text.	**Author and me:** The answer to the question may be found in the text, but the reader may have to combine parts of the text to arrive at an answer. The words in the question may not directly lead the reader to the answer in the text. The reader has to make connections to find an answer. The answer may also be found in a source outside of the text.
Think and search: The answer to the question is embedded within the text in a way that makes it more difficult to find. It may be broken up or require a grasp of multiple ideas across pages or sections of the text.	**On my own:** The answer to the question is not found in the text. The reader must use prior knowledge and personal experiences to answer the question. The reader may even be able to answer the question without having read the text, although text information will enhance the response.

Part B Directions: Copy the questions you will be answering in the space below. Then code the question in the column on the right.

Use the following codes to identify the kinds of questions you are being asked:

R = Right there   A = Author and me

T = Think and search   O = On my own

Question	Code
1.	
2.	
3.	

Ask Questions

Stance Questioning

Directions: Respond to the following questions in order to develop your understanding of the text.

Global Understanding—Being Out and Stepping Into the Text

- What is the overall purpose of the text?

- What is the most important point in the text?

- What details support the most important point?

- How do the text features help support the main idea of the text?

Developing an Interpretation—Being In and Moving Through the Text

- When were you able to infer the feelings or attitudes of any of the people described in the text?

- When were you able to relate concepts or themes to specific information in the text?

- Compare two excerpts of significant information from the text.

- Identify the cause/effect relationship of important events, concepts, or ideas in the text.

- How would the information be different if one of the events or steps described were changed or deleted?

Reflecting on Personal Experiences—Being In and Stepping Out of the Text

- What prior knowledge/personal experiences can you connect to this topic?

- How is the author's point of view on this topic similar to or different from your point of view?

- What other information would you like to learn on this topic?

- What new information have you gained about this topic and why is this information important to you?

Critical Response—Stepping Out and Analyzing the Reading Experience

- How does the author create interest about his or her subject?

- Based on the text, what kind of teacher would the author make? Give specific examples. What does the author believe about his or her subject? How do you know?

Ask Questions

Double-Entry Journal

Directions: As you read, record significant information from the text and your questions about what you have read. Use the following sentence starters to get you started with your questions:

I don't understand when…

Why did…

I'm confused about…

How did…

Quote, summary, or illustration	Questions and wonderings

Ask Questions

Digging Deeper

Directions: Imagine going on an archeological dig to understand text information. Read the text and record key information by copying a significant quote or summarizing important information. Then use the question starters to build your understanding of the concepts or ideas about which you are learning.

Quote or summary of text information	Questions
	I was confused when…
	I want to understand the information about…
	Because…
	I wonder if…
	When I continue reading, I most want to know about…

Ask Questions

Coding for Quality Questioning

Directions: As you read, use the codes below to mark in the margins or on sticky notes next to significant segments of text. Then record your answers to the questions for quality thinking.

T-S = Text-to-Self questioning

T-T = Text-to-Text questioning

T-W = Text-to-World questioning

T-S (Text-to-Self) page_____ and paragraph _____

How does the text connect to your personal experiences?

How does the text connect to your feelings on the topic?

T-T (Text-to-Text) page _____ and paragraph _____

How does the text connect to information that you have read in other texts?

Does this text information confirm or contradict what you have read in other texts about the same topic? Explain.

T-W (Text-to-World) page _____ and paragraph _____

How does the text connect to what you already know about the topic?

How does the text connect to current events?

Ask Questions

Concept and Fact Questions

Directions: Read the text and, on the left, under the heading for concept questions, record questions that require inferences, references to concept knowledge, connections to other texts, or further research. On the right, below the heading for fact questions, record fact-based questions, right-there questions, and questions about vocabulary.

Concept questions	Fact questions

Ask Questions

Question Squares

Directions: Read the information and record significant facts from the text. Then write questions for three audiences: the teacher, the author, and your classmates.

Key topic or concept: _____

Facts related to the topic	Questions for the teacher
Questions for the author	**Questions for the class**

Ask Questions

Questions Before, During, and After

Directions: Record your questions throughout the reading process. Pause at each stage to record speculations and predictions. After you have finished reading, identify more questions and possible answers.

Questions before reading	Speculations
Questions during reading	**Predictions**
Questions after reading	**Possible answers**

Determine Importance

PASSPORT TO COMPREHENSION

Determine Importance—
Main Idea and Supporting Details

Introduction

Secondary-level students must be able to identify the main idea in texts across the curriculum. Identifying the main idea provides the cognitive foundation for questioning, visualizing, connecting to prior knowledge, and many other sophisticated reading strategies. Many students will quickly be able to identify the main idea by previewing the text. Other students will need to read carefully, examine supporting details, and make deductions about the main idea. Still other students will struggle with identifying the main idea and need explicit instruction and modeling in order to master this skill. One of the first things teachers must do in their classrooms each year is diagnose students' abilities in identifying the main idea. Once teachers determine students' needs, they will need to use strategies and instructional approaches that meet the diverse needs of all students. Lessons and activities should reinforce the skills that secondary-level students are presumed to have mastered. These skills include identifying the main idea, retelling, finding evidence to support the main idea, and restating facts and details.

Finding the Main Idea

The main idea is the point that the author wishes to make about a topic. It is the central thought or message that readers need to understand. Students also should understand that the main idea is often *explicit*: the author states the central idea within the text. However, sometimes the main idea is *implicit*; that is, the main idea is not stated anywhere within the text and readers must infer the message from the supporting details. The following paragraphs are examples of both explicit and implicit main ideas:

The main idea is the first sentence followed by details:

> *Clara Barton, known as America's first nurse, was a brave and devoted humanitarian.* While caring for others, she was shot at, got frostbitten fingers, had severe laryngitis twice, burned her hands, and almost lost her eyesight. Yet she continued to care for the sick and injured until she died at the age of 91.

The main idea is in the middle of the paragraph with details on both sides:

> The coral have created a reef where more than 200 kinds of birds and about 1,500 types of fish live. *In fact, Australia's Great Barrier Reef provides a home for many interesting animals.* These include sea turtles, giant clams, crabs, and crown-of-thorns starfish.

The main idea is the last sentence, summarizing the details that came before it:

> Each year, Antarctica spends six months in darkness from mid-March to mid-September. The continent is covered year-round by ice that causes sunlight to reflect off its surface. It never really warms up. In fact, the coldest temperature ever recorded was in Antarctica. *Antarctica has one of the harshest environments in the world.*

Determine Importance— Main Idea and Supporting Details

Finding the Main Idea *(cont.)*

The main idea is not stated in the paragraph and must be inferred from the supporting details:

> The biggest sea horse ever found was over a foot (45 cm) long. Large sea horses live along the coasts of New Zealand, Australia, and California. Smaller sea horses live off the coast of Florida, in the Caribbean Sea, and in the Gulf of Mexico. The smallest adult sea horse ever found was only one-half inch (1.3 cm) long.

In this example the implied main idea is that sea horses' sizes vary based on where they live.

Retelling Key Text Information

The ability to retell is important because it enables students to encapsulate key information as it relates to the main idea and to learn content. Students need to internalize the following questions in order to demonstrate their mastery of retelling:

> What is the key concept or main idea in the text?
>
> What are the important supporting details?
>
> What is extraneous information?
>
> How can I link the important information together?
>
> How can I retell the information in my own words?

Finding Evidence to Support the Main Idea

In order to make sense of texts across the curriculum, students must also be accountable for finding evidence that supports the main idea. The following are some tips for helping students find key textual evidence when reading:

1. Reread the text, skimming and scanning for important information.

2. Reread the headings and subheadings to determine supporting evidence.

3. Look at the text features and read the captions.

4. Reread the introduction and conclusion for generalizations and conceptual information. Compare and contrast supporting paragraphs.

5. Work with a partner to discuss and find evidence from the text.

6. Read multiple texts on the same topic and compare supporting details in order to discover what is most important.

Determine Importance— Main Idea and Supporting Details

Restating Facts and Details

Students must learn to restate facts and supporting details in order to remember important information. Having them categorize facts as they read helps them make inferences about clusters of related words. When necessary, the teacher can give struggling readers the categories before they read and have them sort details or facts into those categories as they read. More capable students can list the facts, categorize, and then reread to see if they missed any information. As students gain independence with this skill, the teacher can have them read short portions of text and identify a category of information and the facts and details that further develop or explain the category. The goal is to help students become readers who automatically sort and organize information in their minds as they read in order to restate the information in a coherent manner. Achieving this goal requires intense strategy instruction and modeling of the strategy by the teacher so that students understand what is expected of them.

Using Graphic Sources

Students at the secondary level will need continuous skill building in using graphic sources. Text that is highly visual and graphic is very motivating. However, it is important that students are able to discern the main idea and supporting details even when previewing, reading, and analyzing graphic texts. Often they will become distracted by highly graphic texts. They may focus on the illustrations, photographs, and charts and thus, fail to come away with an understanding of the main idea of the text. Previewing text can solve this problem. Also, use think alouds to model how to identify and retain important information and ignore extraneous information. In this strategy the teacher vocalizes his or her cognitive processes, or thoughts. While going through a text, the teacher says aloud what he or she is thinking about the main ideas and supporting details. For example, in reading a paragraph on national parks, the teacher might model the think-aloud strategy by saying:

> *As I read the heading of the paragraph, I am alert to the fact that this piece of writing seems to be about national parks. As I continue to look at the page, I see a picture of a man who developed the idea of preserving national parkland. I notice a chart that gives dates when each national park was established. This paragraph seems to be about the early development of national parks. Let's read it to see if that's so...*

Determine Importance—
Main Idea and Supporting Details

Communicating Main Ideas

It is imperative that secondary-level students communicate main ideas. One strategy is to have students read a short piece of text and then work in groups to identify the main idea. After identifying the main idea, each group writes it on a sentence strip and shares it with the class. When they have mastered this skill, they will be able to synthesize key information whenever they are listening and/or reading and articulate the main idea, key concept, or central theme.

Communicating Critical Details

In addition to communicating the main idea, students must be able to communicate the critical details that support it. Main idea and supporting details are a mental construct that students must internalize. Have students analyze and synthesize text information. Show them how analyzing requires them to break the information into details that connect to the main idea. Then show them how synthesizing requires them to connect all of the details by forming a generalization. Have students share their analyses and syntheses frequently in class with partners, small groups, and the whole class in order to gain proficiency.

Using Strategies Independently

The goal of all strategy instruction is that students will be able to select and use strategies independently to meet their needs as readers. Model the strategies included in this section (and in all sections that follow); and when students are ready, allow them to work in groups and with partners to determine the main idea. After diagnosing their proficiencies in determining the main idea, allow students to engage in guided practice with independent reading activities that require them to identify the main idea and supporting details. Expose students to a variety of texts in terms of topic, readability, and complexity of ideas presented.

Determine Importance—
Main Idea and Supporting Details

Strategy 1: SQ3R

Survey, question, read, recite, and review (SQ3R) is an excellent strategy for helping students determine the main idea (Robinson 1970, as described in Irvin 1998).

✓ Begin by having students **survey** the text for organizational structure. Give them a few minutes to look through the chapter, noting the heading and subheadings and looking for introductory and summary paragraphs, boldface type, margin notes, captions, graphs, photos, and illustrations. Research has shown that when students have a strong and accurate awareness of structure, they are better able to determine and retain main ideas and supporting details.

✓ Next, have students convert subheadings into **questions** that they will try to answer as they read. For example, if a chapter subheading is "Similarities Between Frogs and Toads," students should convert it to a question: What are the similarities between frogs and toads?

✓ After forming their questions, students then **read** one section at a time, looking for answers to the questions they asked.

✓ Next, pair students with partners and have them **recite** (or write) a key phrase, summary, or paraphrase of the important information they read by referring to the answers that they generated.

✓ In the **review** stage, have students use graphic organizers or a list of key phrases to reformulate their knowledge for a deeper understanding and to test themselves on what they recall about the chapter.

If you use this method, do it often enough to make it second nature for students. For this strategy to be effective, students should be able to do the steps without having to think about them. (Standards 7.3, 8.2)

Determine Importance— Main Idea and Supporting Details

Strategy 2: Main Idea and Supporting Details

To use this four-step strategy, begin with a paragraph in which the main idea is obvious, even if it is not stated in a topic sentence. The passage must be at students' independent reading levels. The following example of this strategy also helps students understand that there is a difference between the topic of a passage and the main idea.

The Berlin Wall, built by Communists in 1961, split the country of Germany in two. People on the east side of the wall could no longer go to West Germany; people on the west side could no longer go to East Germany. The wall was 20 feet high and made of solid concrete with barbed wire along the top. Soldiers, dogs, and guards in watchtowers kept people from crossing over the wall.

Step 1: Identify the key word(s) in each sentence.

1. Berlin Wall, Communists, Germany
2. people on east side
3. people on west side
4. high, concrete, barbed wire
5. soldiers, dogs, watchtowers

Step 2: Identify the topic (what all the sentences have in common).

The Berlin Wall

Step 3: Write a sentence stating the main idea (based on information from Steps 1 and 2).

The Berlin Wall split Germany and kept apart the people on both sides.

Step 4: If possible, locate a sentence in the paragraph that states the main idea.

"The Berlin Wall, built by the Communists in 1961, split the country of Germany in two."

The Main Idea and Supporting Details activity (page 136) also helps students determine the main idea and evaluate the importance of supporting details. (Standards 5.6, 7.3)

Strategy 3: Examining Graphic Features

To understand the structure of nonfiction texts, students need to be familiar with using graphic elements to help them discover the main idea and supporting details. The activity on page 137 helps them use titles, headings, subheadings, charts, graphs, pictures, and illustrations to discover the main idea. (Standards 7.2, 7.3)

Determine Importance—
Main Idea and Supporting Details

Strategy 4: Previewing the Text to Make Predictions

Another strategy that helps students use graphic features to determine the main idea is to have them preview the chapter and make predictions about what will be important and what might not be important. The activity on page 138 provides practice with this strategy. (Standards 7.3, 7.5)

Strategy 5: A Self-Monitoring Approach to Reading and Thinking (SMART)

Developed by Vaughn and Estes (1986) and further described by Irvin (1998), this simple five-step strategy helps students discover what they don't understand in a text. (Standards 7.3, 8.2)

Step 1: Do I understand?

Students read a paragraph and ask, "Do I totally understand everything in this paragraph?" They place a check in the margin of the text or on a sticky note when they understand and a question mark when they do not.

Step 2: What have I just read?

At the end of each paragraph, students stop to summarize in their own words what they have just read. They can look back at the text during this activity.

Step 3: Does it make sense now?

After students finish reading the text, they return to each paragraph that has a question mark and reread. If it still does not make sense, they move to step 4.

Step 4: Why am I having this trouble?

Students try to pinpoint the problem. Is the difficulty unfamiliar words or concepts? Is the sentence structure too complex? Do they have little background information about the topic? Students need to figure out their specific stumbling blocks before moving to step 5.

Step 5: Where can I get help?

Students should try a variety of aids: glossary, appendix, dictionary, chapter summary, etc. If they are still confused after going through these five steps, they need to ask a classmate or teacher for assistance.

As students become more comfortable with this strategy, make a rule that they cannot ask for help from the teacher unless they can do the following:

- Identify the exact source of their confusion.
- Describe the steps they've already taken on their own to solve the problem.

Determine Importance— Main Idea and Supporting Details

Strategy 6: Text Coding and Main Idea

When students use text coding, they are able to monitor their understanding as they read. Provide students with the following codes:

I = Important

MI = Main Idea (or connects to main idea)

SD = Supporting Detail

Q = Question

As they read, have them mark the text directly or use sticky notes to record the appropriate codes. When they have finished reading, have them use the double-entry journal format to record the words and phrases that correspond with the codes. In the response column, have students identify why the information is important, how the text connects to the main idea, or questions that they have about the text. Use the Text Coding and Main Idea activity (page 139) for this strategy. (Standards 7.3, 8.2)

Strategy 7: Box Web

Using art strategies to represent the main idea and supporting details can be highly motivating especially to struggling readers. Have them use the Box Web activity (page 140) to draw their illustrations of the main idea and four supporting details and to explain how engaging in this activity helps them understand the text information. (Standards 7.3, 7.4)

Strategy 8: Personal Experience and Prior Knowledge

Connecting to personal experience and prior knowledge is a good way to motivate students to find supporting details and retain the information once they have found it. Use the activities on pages 141 and 142 to provide a framework for students to identify the main idea and supporting details and then record them on the left side of the charts. On the right side of the charts, students can respond in a variety of ways by connecting the text to their life experiences or to their prior knowledge of the topic or concept. (Standards 7.3, 7.4)

Strategy 9: Novelty Note Taking

A simple but powerful note-taking technique is to have students use a two-column format (page 143) to record facts from the text on the left side and then reflect on how those facts connect to the main idea on the right side of the journal. After students complete this activity, have them work with a partner to compare the facts they recorded on the right side of their journals and to discuss the similarities and differences among the connections they made. (Standards 7.3, 7.4)

Determine Importance— Main Idea and Supporting Details

Strategy 10: Retelling and Reacting

Retelling is a critical component of identifying the main idea and supporting details. Provide students with the Retelling and Reacting activity (page 144) and have them restate in their own words the important events in the text on the left side of the chart. Then have them react on the right side of the chart by identifying how the retold events connect to their own lives, reveal the main idea, or provide important information. Give students the opportunity to deduce the main idea by re-examining the chart. (Standards 7.3, 7.4)

Strategy 11: Tic-Tac-Toe and Details

Give students a blank copy of the Tic-Tac-Toe and Details activity (page 145). Have them read a text and then fill in the details from the text on the tic-tac-toe game card. Then have them switch papers with a partner and give them tokens. Have partners read the text. Every time they find one of the details on the game card, instruct them to place a token (page 146) on the appropriate box. The first person to place three tokens in a row horizontally, vertically, or diagonally wins. Close by having students complete Part C. (Standards 7.3, 7.4)

Determine Importance—
Main Idea and Supporting Details

Main Idea and Supporting Details

Directions: Identify the main idea and supporting details. Make sure to evaluate the importance of the supporting details.

Concept or topic being studied: _____

Title of the text: _____

Main idea: _____

Identify three supporting details and rate their importance in understanding the main idea.

1 = Very important

2 = Somewhat important

3 = Not very important

Supporting details	Importance rating
1.	
2.	
3.	

Do the supporting details help you better understand the topic that you are studying? Explain.

_____

_____

_____

_____

Determine Importance— Main Idea and Supporting Details

Examining Graphic Features

Directions: Examine the graphic features of the text and determine the main idea.

Chapter or section title: _____

Headings and subheadings: _____

_____

_____

_____

Graphic features (charts, graphs, pictures, etc.):

Identify	Describe
1.	
2.	
3.	

Based on your examination of the graphic features, what is the main idea? Write the main idea in your own words.

_____

_____

_____

How did examining the graphic features help you identify the main idea?

_____

_____

_____

Determine Importance— Main Idea and Supporting Details

Previewing the Text to Make Predictions

Directions: Answer the following questions to determine the main idea.

What is the text length and structure?	What are the important headings and subheadings?
What should I be sure to read and in what order should I read it?	What parts of the text should I read very carefully?
What parts of the text do not look important? What should I skip or ignore?	How will the text connect to my prior knowledge?

What is the main idea? _____

How do I know? _____

_____

_____

_____

Determine Importance— Main Idea and Supporting Details

Text Coding and Main Idea

Directions: As you read, use the following codes to mark on a sticky note next to words or phrases that reveal the main idea. Then use the chart below to record the words or phrases and to reflect on how they show the main idea or supporting details.

I = Important

MI = Main Idea (or connects to main idea)

SD = Supporting Detail

Q = Question (This seems important, but I am not sure how…)

Words or phrases that reveal the main idea and supporting details	Response (Choose from the sentence starters below to get you started on your response.) • This information is important because… • This information connects to the main idea because… • This supporting detail is important because… • I am not sure how this connects to the main idea but…

Determine Importance—
Main Idea and Supporting Details

Box Web

Directions: Draw pictures of the main idea in the center box and four supporting details in the outer boxes.

Supporting detail	**Supporting detail**
	Main idea	
Supporting detail	**Supporting detail**

How does illustrating the main idea and supporting details help you understand the information?

_____

_____

_____

Determine Importance—
Main Idea and Supporting Details

Personal Experience and Prior Knowledge—Part 1

Directions: Connect the main idea and supporting details to your prior knowledge.

Main idea	Prior knowledge about the main idea

Supporting detail 1:	Prior knowledge or questions:
Supporting detail 2:	**Prior knowledge or questions:**
Supporting detail 3:	**Prior knowledge or questions:**

How will connecting to your prior knowledge help you remember the main idea and supporting details?

_____

_____

_____

Determine Importance—
Main Idea and Supporting Details

Personal Experience and Prior Knowledge—Part 2

Directions: Connect the main ideas and supporting details in the text to your own life by writing the main idea in the space provided. Then write four details that support the main idea on the left side of the chart. In the response column, answer all the guiding questions for each detail.

Main idea: _____

Supporting details	Response • How does this supporting detail connect to my life? • How does this supporting detail further explain the main idea? • How is this supporting detail important to me? Why will I need this information?

Determine Importance— Main Idea and Supporting Details

Novelty Note Taking

Directions: Record facts and details from the text in the left column. In the right column, record your reactions to each fact or detail by answering the following questions:

1. How do the details connect to the main idea?
2. Is the author's approach to the subject novel, or unique? How?
3. What further questions do you have?

Facts and details from the text	Reactions

Determine Importance—
Main Idea and Supporting Details

Retelling and Reacting

Directions: In the left column, retell four important events or ideas from the text. In the right column, record your reactions by answering the following questions for each event or idea. Then record what you feel is the main idea from your chart.

1. How do these events or ideas relate to my life?
2. How do these events or ideas reveal the main idea?
3. Why are these events or ideas important for me to know?

Important events/ideas	Reactions

What is the main idea? _____

Determine Importance—
Main Idea and Supporting Details

Tic-Tac-Toe and Details

Part A Directions: Read the text and place one detail in each of the boxes below.

Part B Directions: Switch papers with a partner. Read the text, and use the tokens on page 146 to cover a detail every time you find one in the text that is written on your paper. The first student to place three tokens in a row horizontally, vertically, or diagonally wins.

Part C Directions: Use the details to make a generalization about the main idea of the article. Write your statement on the back of this paper.

Determine Importance— Main Idea and Supporting Details

Tic-Tac-Toe and Details *(cont.)*

Directions: Cut out the tokens for use with the Tic-Tac-Toe activity on page 145.

Determine Importance—
Text Structures

Introduction

Authors use different structures to organize and present information in order to affect the reader in different ways. Well-written text reflects unity and coherence because the ideas are organized and the relationships among ideas are made clear. However, students often encounter "inconsiderate" text in which the ideas are not presented clearly and the relationships among ideas are vague, disorganized, or nonexistent. If students understand how structural patterns are used, they will easily be able to make sense of well-written text. In addition, if students encounter "inconsiderate" text, they will know why the information seems inaccessible, and they will be able to analyze the text by using their knowledge of structural patterns.

Authors of nonfiction texts utilize many different structures, all unified by the fact that they are organized around topics and their details. There are five generally recognized structures or patterns in content textbooks:

1. **Chronological Order** (also known as *logical, sequential,* or *order and sequence*)
2. **Compare and Contrast**
3. **Cause and Effect**
4. **Proposition and Support** (also known as *problem and solution*)
5. **Progression of Ideas** (also known as *description and listing* or *description and collection*)

The authors of nonfiction use these patterns to arrange and connect ideas. Most writers typically employ several structural patterns in the same text. Only occasionally is the entire book organized around just one pattern.

Chronological, Logical, and Sequential Order

When authors want to show a sequence of events, ideas, or steps, they will use narrative, chronological, or sequential order as a text structure. Often, chronological text in social studies will tell the story of a battle, the life of a historical figure, or the formation of a new nation. Sequential text in science will outline the steps of an experiment. In math, sequential text will describe the steps of a particular problem-solving process. Make sure to model how to identify sequential order and how to apply this structural approach to their own writing. Signal words that indicate chronological text include *next, first, last, second, another, then, before, additionally, earlier, later,* and *finally.*

Determine Importance— Text Structures

Compare and Contrast

Often authors will want to show the similarities and differences among various topics or ideas and therefore will use a compare-and-contrast structural pattern. For example, a social studies text may delineate the similarities and differences between the American Indians and the European colonists or among fascist, democratic, socialist, and communist forms of government. A science text may compare various chemical reactions or various geological time periods. A math text may compare different ways of solving a particular kind of problem. Compare and contrast may involve an element of analysis because the writer may include an evaluation of which method, approach, or idea is better. Astute readers need to be aware of how their feelings about the topic are being shaped. Signal words for compare and contrast include:

however	by contrast	opposites
while	yet	different than
but	in comparison	as well as
rather	although	likewise
most	whereas	on the other hand
unlike	similar to	conversely
like	similarly	instead

Cause and Effect

When authors want to show the relationship between events and consequences, they will often choose a cause-and-effect structure. Often there is a discernible if/then pattern that the reader will be able to recognize. It is important to teach students that even though causes have related effects, there is often a slightly more complicated element to this structure in which the effects are often the "cause" of a new problem which has a new "effect." Cause-and-effect structures show readers the relationship between ideas and events. Critical readers should be taught how to determine when a writer is making illogical leaps or attempting to assign a cause-and-effect relationship without adequate support. Signal words for cause and effect include:

consequently	then… so	therefore
because	for this reason	as a result
since	on account of	thereby
nevertheless	thus	leads to
due to	so that	consequently
this led to	if… then	

Determine Importance— Text Structures

Proposition and Support

When texts are arranged in a proposition-and-support structure, the writer proposes a proposition, hypothesis, theory, or problem and offers examples to support the theory or solve the problem. For example, the writer may propose a neighborhood cleanup. Support for this idea may include: 1) A neighborhood cleanup will get the community involved and interacting with each other in a positive way; 2) More people working together will help get the job done quickly; 3) If one community cleans up its neighborhood, maybe other communities will follow suit. Setting a good example will ultimately make a cleaner Earth.

The proposition-and-support structure is great for persuasive pieces of writing, including editorials. Writers may include the pros and cons of the solution. This approach relies heavily on persuasive techniques because the writer often has a particular solution in mind and will craft the text to prove his or her solution. Critical readers need to be taught how to recognize bias and how to evaluate whether an argument is balanced. Signal words include those used for cause and effect, as well as *propose, conclude, research shows, the evidence is, a reason for, a solution, the problem* or *the question.*

Progression of Ideas

When writers use a progression-of-ideas structure, they list key features about the topic and elaborate on each one. For example, a social studies text may list various features of a geographic/political region such as India or Saudi Arabia. These features may include government, religion, currency, economy, language, etc. A science text may list various characteristics of a particular species. Readers need to become aware of the feature/details pattern of a progression-of-ideas format. Often this pattern is offset by headings and subheadings. Progression of ideas is intended to teach the reader about the topic. Critical readers then need to piece together the relationships among ideas.

Recognizing Structural Patterns

Model how to determine text structure, author's purpose, and reasons for using specific structures. Because authors often use a combination of two or more structures, it is not always clear which structure the author chose. Share your confusions and questions so students recognize how challenging the identification of text structure can be. Emphasize that learning about text structure helps readers understand text and learn how to use various structures in their own writing. Students can identify text structures in small groups and eventually on their own. Allow them to apply this knowledge to their own writing. Repeated use will build their independence with analyzing and using different structures.

Determine Importance— Text Structures

Strategy 1: Description Tree

Use the Description Tree (page 153) to have students brainstorm details related to one topic. For example, if students are going to brainstorm about their summer vacations, they would write "summer vacation" in the empty box at the top of the organizer. Then they would select two aspects of summer vacation, such as soccer camp and a trip to the beach. As they proceed in completing the graphic organizer, they would continue to generate details that are more and more specific. Finally, they would use the ideas from their graphic organizers to write paragraphs or essays about their summer vacations. You can also use this organizer to have students identify details in a text written in a progression-of-ideas pattern. (Standards 7.3, 7.4)

Strategy 2: Compare/Contrast Organizer

Collect calendar pages with pictures of places, people, and things. Once you have several calendar pages, conduct the following compare-and-contrast activity. Divide students into groups of four. Give each group two calendar pages and the Compare/Contrast Organizer I (page 154) and have them work together to identify the similarities and differences between the two pages. Then give each group three different calendar pages and have them complete the Compare/Contrast Organizer II (page 155). Have students share their organizers. Then introduce students to a compare-and-contrast text and have them apply their skills to the text. This strategy can be used to compare a variety of subjects, such as comparing and contrasting authors, historical events, geographical regions, or animal species. (Standards 7.3, 7.4)

Strategy 3: Comparison Matrix

Use the organizer on page 156 to have students list as many features of fruit as they can (sweet, nutritious, grows on trees, juicy, textured, etc.) in the left column. Then show students several different kinds of fruit and record them in the top part of the chart. Discuss with students each piece of fruit and its corresponding features, placing a check in the appropriate boxes if the fruit exemplifies a particular feature. Make the connection to text by reading information that identifies the features of a particular topic, comparing similar topics against a list of features. For example, students can identify the features of the American Revolutionary War and then compare this war directly to the War of 1812, the Civil War, WWI, and WWII by using the comparison matrix technique. (Standards 7.3, 7.4)

Strategy 4: Cause-and-Effect Organizer

Have students recall events from their mornings, such as the ride to school or eating breakfast, and use the Cause-and-Effect Organizer (page 157) to identify the cause-and-effect relationships connected with their morning memories. Be sure to have them read a cause-and-effect text and apply their knowledge of these relationships to their reading. The examples on page 151 show how students understand cause and effect in their own lives. (Standards 7.3, 7.4)

Determine Importance—
Text Structures

Strategy 4: Cause-and-Effect Organizer *(cont.)*

Cause		Effect
I come home and finish my homework before I watch TV in the afternoon.	✔	My homework is always done and then I have the rest of the night to relax.
I practice the piano for 30 minutes every day.	✔	I learned a very difficult song on the piano and performed it for my family at a recital.
I gave the new seed water, air, and light.	✔	It will grow into a large plant.

Strategy 5: Sequence Chain

Give students several simple topics or "how-to" ideas and have them complete a sequence chain (page 158). Topics may include: brushing your teeth, making a sandwich, making an ice cream sundae, etc. Encourage students to be as detailed and specific as possible. After they share their "how-to" creations with the class, have them read a sequential text and identify the steps or events with great detail and precision and fill out another sequence chain. (Standards 7.3, 7.4)

Strategy 6: Problem/Solution Organizer

Tell students that they need to plan out a project in which they identify a real audience, identify a problem that impacts that audience, and brainstorm solutions to the problem. For example, identify with students many ways that they could positively impact their school or neighborhood communities, such as cleaning up litter, planting trees, or fixing playground equipment. Discuss the possible pros and cons of the solution(s). Provide them with the Problem/Solution Organizer (page 159). (Standards 7.3, 7.4)

Strategy 7: Proposition/Support Organizer

An alternative to the Problem/Solution Organizer is the Proposition/Support Organizer (page 160). Students can do a similar activity in which they plan a community service project, but in this case they make a proposal about a community problem and offer support for that proposal. Students can develop a different proposal as long as they include a specific proposition, supporting details, and a conclusion. (Standards 7.3, 7.4)

Determine Importance—
Text Structures

Strategy 8: Never-ending Narratives

Give students a choice of various topics that require a chronological pattern and have the first student write one sentence about one topic. (You could begin with the first or last person in each row and have him or her pass his or her paper to the student behind or in front of him or her.) Then have the next student pass his or her paper to the next student who will add the next event. Encourage students to vary their transitions, using words other than "next" and "then." Have students continue passing papers for about 15 minutes. Stop and have some students share what has been written thus far. Ask them about the quality of the narratives and whether adding more information would improve the stories. Remind students that authors need to be judicious when adding events to stories. (Standards 7.3, 7.4)

Strategy 9: Time Line

A time line helps students show a sequence in a process or a series of events. It requires them to place one event or idea after another according to the order in which they occur. Time lines can be used in social studies to connect specific dates with events. You might have students practice using a time line by instructing them to place the events of their lives on a time line (page 161). Then they can analyze a chronological or sequential text to determine the order of important events. (Standards 7.3, 7.4)

Strategy 10: Structure Words

Divide students into groups and give them small segments of text in which the structure words have been deleted. Have them refer to the Structure Words activity (page 162) to identify the best words to "sew" the text back together and to help them identify the structure that the author chose to use. The simple example below demonstrates how useful this activity can be in teaching students the significance of structure words. (Standards 7.3, 7.4)

> *A tree will undergo many changes throughout the year as the seasons change. _____*
> *(First), the leaves of a tree turn into brilliant colors in fall. They also begin to fall off the tree.*
> *_____ (Then) winter brings cold weather and tree limbs are bare. Most trees are*
> *without any leaves at all. _____ (Next), springtime means that buds are growing*
> *and trees are beginning to bloom again. _____ (Finally), summer months with*
> *lots of sunshine mean that trees continue to grow leaves and remain green. This cycle occurs each*
> *year.*

Strategy 11: Analysis of Text Structure

Collect articles, passages, or texts that are written in each of the structural patterns studied. Pair students with a partner and give each pair one type of pattern. The pair will read the text, determine the structure, explain how that pattern helps the author achieve his or her purpose, and then look for any flaws in the structure. Use the Analysis of Text Structure activity (page 163) for this strategy. The partners should then report their findings to the class. (Standards 7.3, 7.4)

Determine Importance—
Text Structures

Description Tree

Directions: Identify the details in a specific text or plan your description of a topic.

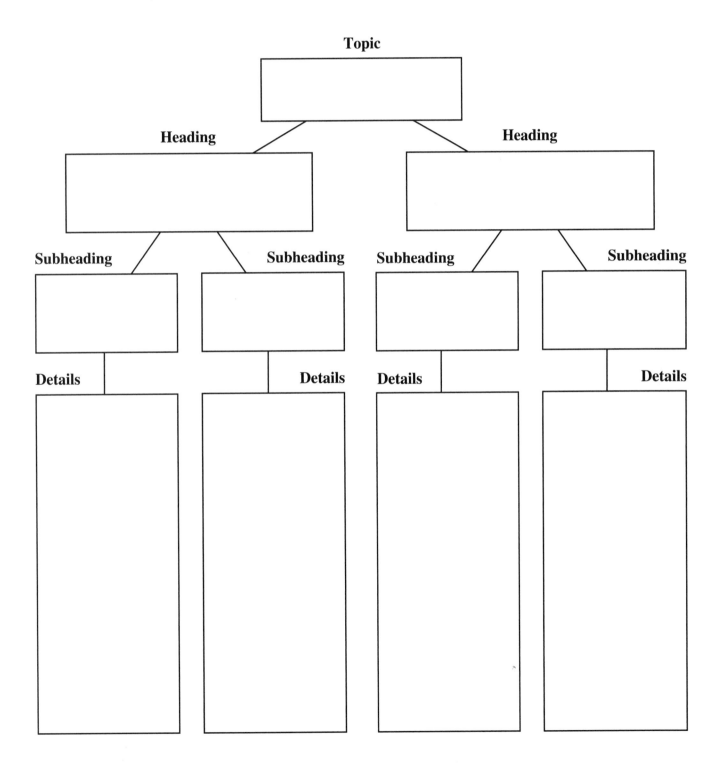

Topic

Heading   **Heading**

Subheading   **Subheading**   **Subheading**   **Subheading**

Details   **Details**   **Details**   **Details**

Determine Importance— Text Structures

Compare/Contrast Organizer—Part 1

Directions: List the similarities and differences between the two things being compared.

Two things being compared:

1. _____

2. _____

Differences	Similarities

Determine Importance— Text Structures

Compare/Contrast Organizer—Part 2

Directions: List the similarities and differences between each of the three things being compared.

Three things being compared:

1. _____

2. _____

3. _____

Determine Importance—
Text Structures

Comparison Matrix

Directions: As you read, list the features or characteristics of the topic(s) about which you are reading in the left column. Then list the things being compared across the top of the chart. Place a check in each box in which the things being compared match the feature or characteristic listed.

Things being compared → Features used for comparison ↓					
1.					
2.					
3.					
4.					
5.					
6.					
7.					
8.					
9.					
10.					

Determine Importance— Text Structures

Cause-and-Effect Organizer

Directions: Identify the cause-and-effect relationships in the text.

Cause   Effect

Determine Importance—
Text Structures

Sequence Chain

Directions: Trace the events or steps described in the text.

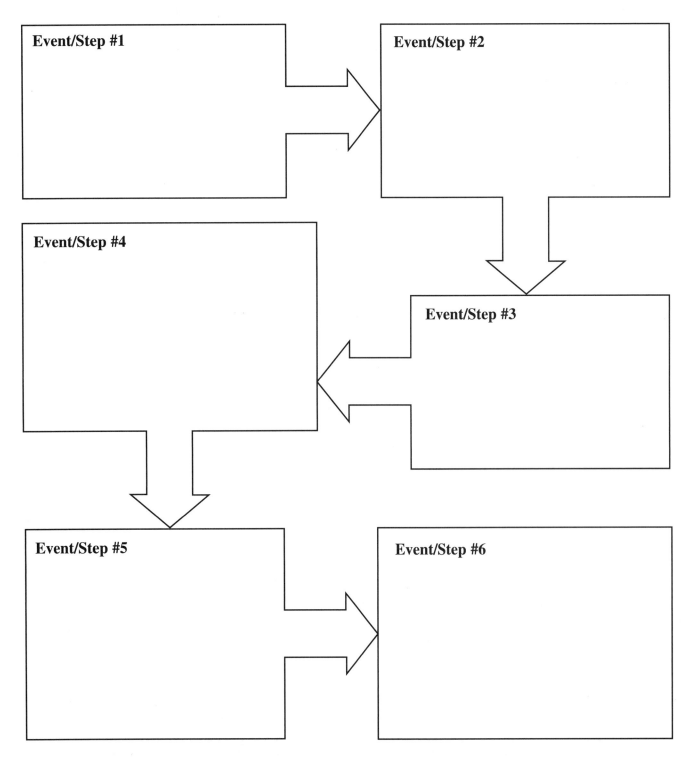

Event/Step #1

Event/Step #2

Event/Step #4

Event/Step #3

Event/Step #5

Event/Step #6

Determine Importance—
Text Structures

Problem/Solution Organizer

Directions: Identify the problem and solution described in the text, as well as the pros and cons of the solution.

Problem:

Solution:

Pros	Cons

STRATEGIES AND SKILLS

Determine Importance— Text Structures

Proposition/Support Organizer

Directions: Identify the proposition, supporting details, and conclusion for your proposal or from the text.

Proposition thesis:

Supporting idea #1:

Supporting idea #2:

Supporting idea #3:

Conclusion:

Determine Importance—
Text Structures

Time Line

Directions: Use this timeline to show sequence in a series of events.

Topic

Determine Importance—
Text Structures

Structure Words

Directions: Use the following chart to guide you in completing the activity.

Pattern	Structure words
Progression of ideas	for example, for instance, another, specifically, besides, also, in addition, in particular, particularly, moreover, furthermore
Cause and effect	consequently, therefore, thus, as a result, however, hence, thereby, leads to, if/then
Compare and contrast	however, on the other hand, but, by contrast, yet, unlike, like, in comparison, although, whereas, similar to, different from, similarly
Chronological, sequential	next, first, last, second, another, then, furthermore, also, additionally, in the first place, in conclusion
Proposition and support	most importantly, in support, first, next, last, in conclusion, a solution, propose

1. As you read, copy two sentences that use structure words. _____

    _____

    _____

    _____

    _____

    _____

2. What structure is the author using? How do you know? _____

    _____

    _____

    _____

    _____

    _____

Determine Importance—
Text Structures

Analysis of Text Structure

Directions: Analyze the author's use of text structure.

Possible Structures	
Progression of ideas	Chronological, sequential
Compare and contrast	Proposition and support
Cause and effect	

1. What is the author's purpose?

_____

_____

_____

2. Which structure is the author using? How do you know?

_____

_____

_____

3. How does the structure help the author achieve his or her purpose?

_____

_____

_____

4. Are there any flaws in the structure? Explain.

_____

_____

_____

_____

_____

_____

_____

_____

Determine Importance— Text Structures

Introduction

Text organizers are intended to enhance the text and appeal to the reader. Text organizers include chapter titles, headings and subheadings, unique typeface, graphic features, and topic and summary sentences. By the time students reach middle school and high school, they need to be able to evaluate whether the author's text organizers enhance or detract from the text. Such critical thinking is the foundation for high levels of reading comprehension.

Chapter Titles

Chapter titles should provide clear information regarding the main idea of the entire reading selection. Authors state the main idea in just a word or a short phrase and let the reader know what information is contained in the subsequent passage. This helps readers sort significant data from data that is less important. Often chapter titles are accompanied by a picture, illustration, photograph, brief explanation, or a quote that further expands the information the author wants the reader to gain. As students are reading the entire selection, they should think about how the headings, subheadings, topic and summary sentences, facts, and details all work together to support and elaborate upon the chapter title.

Using Headings and Subheadings

Informational writers organize their information under headings and subheadings. One way to help students make sense of headings and subheadings is to have them turn the information into a question and instruct them to read for the purpose of answering the question. For example, if the heading is "Photosynthesis and Its Effects on the Environment," students could convert this information into the question, "What is photosynthesis and how does it affect the environment?"

Using Typeface

Publishers of nonfiction materials use a variety of fonts in different typefaces and sizes to signal importance in a text. Typeface can be large, small, colorful, boldface, italicized, squiggly, 3-D, bubbly, cartoon-like, or bulleted. Typeface may reveal importance, but it can also reveal the tone, message, or intent of the text. A change in font, boldface print, or italicized words often show the main ideas or important information. For example, a simple sentence's main idea can be changed with a change in typeface:

- She did not like broccoli. (Main idea: All words are equally important.)

- She did *not* like broccoli. (Main idea: Not liking broccoli is emphasized.)

- She did not like *broccoli*. (Main idea: She does like other vegetables.)

Determine Importance— Text Structures

Using Typeface *(cont.)*

Teaching students how to evaluate typeface is a critical component in helping them identify important information. Some questions that may help students include:

- What inferences can you make about the topics in the text based on the style of the typeface?

- How could the typeface be improved?

- What do you think the author wants you to think or believe about the topic as result of reading the typeface?

Using Graphic Features

Illustrations, photos, diagrams, maps, tables, graphs, and charts all add meaning to a passage. They provide readers with alternative means for visualizing, mentally organizing, and remembering the information they have read. Good publishers try to present these graphic features in a colorful and visually pleasing manner to strengthen reader interest. Graphic features also enhance text through various forms of media. Magazines, advertisements, and the Internet all boast a huge variety of graphic features designed to shape and sometimes manipulate our understanding of the information. It is critical that we teach students how to evaluate whether text features enhance or detract from text information. Some questions that may help students include:

- How do these graphic features help you understand the text?

- What graphic features are missing?

- How would the addition of charts, maps, diagrams, etc., aid your understanding of the text?

Determine Importance— Text Structures

Examining Topic and Summary Sentences

Topic and summary sentences are usually generalizations that reveal the main idea at the beginning or end of a paragraph or passage. Often the entire meaning can be gained from those two sentences alone. Understanding how authors use generalizations and specific details to construct paragraphs will help students organize the text information cognitively. Questions to help students make sense of topic and summary sentences include:

How does the topic sentence support the main idea of the entire piece of text?

How does the summary sentence support or connect to the main idea of the entire piece of text?

What are the facts and details within the paragraph?

How do these facts and details support the topic sentence?

How do these facts and details lead to the summary sentence?

Using Strategies Independently

Students must be adept at using text organizers to preview text, to read text comprehensively, and to review information. Model how to use text organizers for each of these purposes. Allow students to work in small groups or with partners to build their proficiencies in using text organizers to make meaning of the information. Make sure that they are able to use these skills independently.

Strategy 1: Text Organizer Scavenger Hunt

Divide students into groups of four. Instruct them to use a blank sheet of paper to identify each text organizer in the chapter and whether it connects directly to the chapter title. The first group to finish wins the scavenger hunt. (Standard 7.5)

Strategy 2: Using the Chapter Title Before, During, and After Reading

Provide students with a copy of a text selection in which the title has been deleted or covered up. Have them read the text information carefully, noting headings, subheadings, and graphic features. Challenge the class to think of as many possible chapter titles as they can. Write their suggestions on the board and have them vote on the one that seems to best represent the information in the text. Reveal the title that the author chose and ask students to determine which title best suits the text, theirs or the author's. Ask them to provide ample justification for their selection either orally or in writing. Conclude the activity by having students read the text again to complete the organizer on page 171. (Standards 5.4, 7.5)

Determine Importance—
Text Structures

Strategy 3: Converting Headings and Subheadings into Questions

Having students convert headings and subheadings into questions is a simple way to get them to recognize the importance of these text organizers. At first, they will need your guidance in making questions. For example, if a heading is "Reptilian Habitats," some students may not automatically know to create the question, "What are reptilian habitats?" The best way to assist students is to remind them of the 5 Ws + H. Then give them a number of headings and subheadings and have them convert them into questions in a whole-group setting, with a partner, and finally, independently. The Headings and Subheadings activity (page 172) gives students practice with changing headings and subheadings into questions and then answering those questions. (Standards 5.1, 8.2)

Strategy 4: Prediction Chart

Filling out a Prediction Chart is a strategy that will help students focus on the text, its organization, and what to expect. In the first column of the chart, write in the heading of the chapter you are examining. In the second column, "My Prediction," students make predictions based on the heading. Working as a whole group, brainstorm with students what a reasonable prediction would be, based on the subject of the textbook, the title of the chapter, and the heading. Record this information on a transparency made from page 173 or on the board. As you are recording, be sure to ask students to tell why they would make this prediction. This provides verification of their prior knowledge, and also leads students' thought processes to other knowledge. The last column, "What Happened," is where the prediction is confirmed or disputed after they have read the text. (Standards 5.1, 7.5)

PREDICTION CHART (sample)

Chapter Title: _____Protection Against Disease_____

Heading Title	My Prediction	What Happened
What types of microbes are there? How do microbes spread?	It's going to tell me which microbes cause which diseases. It's going to tell me how people can get these diseases.	Viruses cause colds, chicken pox, measles, and rabies. Bacteria cause strep throat and food poisoning. Fungi cause athlete's foot and ringworm. Insects and animals, contaminated water, and spoiled or contaminated food spread disease.

Determine Importance— Text Organizers

Strategy 5: Bold the "Golden" Words

Inform students that important words are boldfaced or italicized in certain kinds of text. These words are usually key terms with definitions that are critical for students to know if they are to comprehend the text. You may want to call these words the "golden" words of the text. For practice, provide students with text in which important words are not boldfaced or italicized and challenge them to underline, circle, or highlight the golden words. Have them complete the task independently and then share their texts with a partner. The pairs should discuss whether each partner selected the same words. As a variation, have students write expository text about a given topic and write the golden words on a separate sheet of paper. Instruct them to switch papers with a partner and have their classmate identify the key words. Have students discuss and justify their selections as a conclusion to the activity. (Standards 5.1, 5.3)

Strategy 6: Identifying Topic Sentences

Have students select several topic sentences from a piece of expository writing and record them on the Identifying Topic Sentences activity (page 174). Next, have them identify key words, phrases, or concepts from the topic sentences that they chose. Finally, have students create new topic sentences and experiment with capturing the key ideas and concepts in those topic sentences. As an extension, have students share their topic sentences in small groups and choose the best one. (Standards 5.1, 7.2)

Strategy 7: Selecting Summary Sentences

Have students select several summary sentences from a piece of expository writing and record them on the Selecting Summary Sentences activity (page 175). Next, have students identify key words, phrases, or concepts from the summary sentences that they chose. Finally, have them create new summary sentences and experiment with capturing the key ideas and concepts in those sentences. As an extension, have students share their summary sentences in small groups and choose the best one. (Standards 5.1, 7.2)

Determine Importance— Text Organizers

Strategy 8: Evaluating Text Organizers and Graphic Features

Explicitly teaching students to evaluate text organizers is very important if students are to be critical consumers of various kinds of media. They will encounter a wide range of text organizers on the Internet and in textbooks, magazines, advertisements, and other forms of print media. Use a coding system like the one found on the Evaluating Text Organizers activity (page 176). Have them write an explanation of the rating that they chose to give the organizer and share their justification with the whole class or with a partner. Instruct students to evaluate the color, size, content, and placement of the text organizer. Have them think about the ways in which the author or text publisher is trying to shape or manipulate their understanding of the text.

Then have students focus on the graphic features of texts, evaluating the author's choice of features. The Evaluating Graphic Features activity (page 177) can be used for this strategy. (Standards 5.1, 7.2)

Strategy 9: Evaluating Author's Purpose

Thinking about the author's intent is essential for students to become critical readers. Have them use the Evaluating Author's Purpose activity (page 178) to identify the text organizers and determine what the author wants them to think, feel, or believe about the topic. For example, if students are reading about westward expansion, the author may show a map of the United States with the most popular routes marked on the map. There may also be illustrations of covered wagons and other supplies that people took with them on their way west. The reader may conclude that the author wants the audience to have some sense of the distance that people traveled west, the kinds of terrain they encountered, and the crude and limited materials and supplies they possessed. The reader may determine that the author wanted him or her to understand the pioneers' experience more realistically. (Standards 5.1, 5.6)

Strategy 10: Choosing the Right Text Organizers

Students need to realize that too many text organizers can prove distracting and confusing to readers. Provide students with a variety of texts that have many graphic features and text organizers. Distribute the Choosing the Right Text Organizer activity (page 179) and have students look for those text organizers that detract from important information. They must then justify their recommendations to delete or modify those text organizers. This strategy requires students to think about the importance of designing text organizers carefully. (Standards 5.1, 5.6)

Determine Importance—
Text Organizers

Strategy 11: Comparing Two Texts

Comparing texts is a good way to further extend students' abilities to think critically about text and to evaluate the effectiveness of text organizers. Pair students with a partner and provide them with at least two different texts. Distribute the Comparing Two Texts activity (page 180), and have the pairs use the rating system to evaluate the effectiveness of the first piece of text. They should follow the same procedure for the second text. Encourage them to think about how the color, size, placement, and content of the organizer helps or hinders their understanding of text information. Finally, have them give an overall effectiveness rating to the texts and decide which author did a better job including text organizers. (Standards 5.5, 7.2)

Strategy 12: Add a Text Organizer

Provide students with nonfiction text that does not have any text organizers. Review the different text organizers: chapter titles, headings, subheadings, charts, diagrams, graphs, maps, illustrations, photographs, cartoons, captions, and typeface. Instruct students to find places in the text where a text organizer would really help them better understand the text. Invite students to create a few of the text organizers for the text. If they decide to create graphs, charts, or diagrams, you may have to take them to the school library to do further research on the topic. Use the Add a Text Organizer activity (page 181) for this strategy. (Standards 5.5, 7.2)

Strategy 13: Investigating the Internet

Having students evaluate appropriate websites and Web pages will help them apply their critical reading skills to the use of technology. Make sure you work closely with the computer teacher or the school librarian to ensure that all sites are appropriate for students. Have students examine how the color, size, shape, movement, content, and placement of the text organizers on websites influence their understanding of the text information. (Standards 5.6, 7.2)

Determine Importance—
Text Organizers

Using the Chapter Title Before, During, and After Reading

Directions: Think about the chapter title and its connection to the main ideas and supporting details of the chapter before, during, and after you read the text.

Chapter title: _____

Before reading: Read the chapter title. Make a list of questions that you have about the topic in the chapter title.	**During reading:** Take notes about the information that you are learning.
After reading: What did you learn? Answer the questions that you asked before reading.	**Questions for future research:** What questions do you still have about the topic?

Determine Importance— Text Organizers

Converting Headings and Subheadings into Questions

Directions: Change two of the headings or subheadings in the text into questions, answer the questions, and write a reaction to the answers.

Heading/Subheading as a question: _____

_____

Answer: _____

_____

_____

_____

_____

_____

Reaction: (How does this relate to my life? What further questions do I have?) _____

_____

_____

_____

_____

Heading/Subheading as a question: _____

_____

Answer:_____

_____

_____

_____

_____

_____

Reaction: (How does this relate to my life? What further questions do I have?)_____

_____

_____

_____

_____

Determine Importance—
Text Organizers

Prediction Chart

Directions: Using the title and headings from the text, predict what the chapter will be about. Read the text and then write what happened.

Chapter title: _____

Heading	My prediction	What happened

Determine Importance—
Text Organizers

Identifying Topic Sentences

Directions: Experiment with creating new topic sentences for the text you read.

Current topic sentence	Key words, phrases, or concepts in the topic sentence	New topic sentence

Determine Importance—
Text Organizers

Selecting Summary Sentences

Directions: Experiment with creating new summary sentences for the text you read.

Current summary sentence	Key words, phrases, or concepts in the summary sentence	New summary sentence

Determine Importance— Text Organizers

Evaluating Text Organizers

Directions: Use the following rating codes to evaluate the text organizers you encounter. Write an explanation of your rating in the chart provided below.

I = Important   **F** = Flashy but not important

LI = Limited importance   **X** = Interesting but not important

Text organizer	Rating	Explanation

Determine Importance—
Text Organizers

Evaluating Graphic Features

Directions: Evaluate the author's choice of graphic features.

Describe the graphic features (illustrations, photographs, captions, charts, graphs, maps, etc.)	Evaluation • How does this graphic feature support my understanding of the main idea and/or supporting details? • How could the graphic features have improved my understanding of the main idea and/or supporting details?

Determine Importance—
Text Organizers

Evaluating Author's Purpose

Directions: Evaluate the author's purpose for choosing text organizers by filling out this chart.

Text organizer	Inference about the author's purpose	Evaluation: Did the author achieve his/her purpose? Explain.

Determine Importance—
Text Organizers

Choosing the Right Text Organizer

Directions: Read the text carefully, looking for text organizers that detract from the important information. In the chart below, write recommendations to the author in the left column and justify your recommendation in the right column.

Recommendation for deleting or changing a text organizer	Justification: Explain how this addition, deletion, or modification makes the information clearer.

Why is it important for an author to design text organizers carefully? _____

_____

_____

_____

_____

_____

_____

Determine Importance— Text Organizers

Comparing Two Texts

Directions: Use the following chart to compare the text organizers of two different pieces of text.

Effectiveness Rating

3 = Text organizer was highly informative. It taught me a lot about the main idea.

2 = Text organizer was somewhat informative. I learned a little more about the main idea.

1 = Text organizer was not informative. I did not learn any more about the main idea.

Main idea of text #1	Main idea of text #2

Text #1   Text #2

Text organizers	Effectiveness rating	Text organizers	Effectiveness rating

Overall Rating of Text #1 _____

Overall Rating of Text #2 _____

Determine Importance—
Text Organizers

Add a Text Organizer

Directions: Read a nonfiction text that does not have any text organizers. Find the important information and record it in the left column of the chart. Then think of an illustration, chart, graph, map, or other text organizer that would enhance the text and describe or illustrate your idea in the right column.

Important text information	Your idea for a text organizer

Determine Importance—Using Parts of the Book

Introduction

Nonfiction works focus on a particular topic and are intended to provide factual information through text and visual images. Unlike fictional works that may be based on fact but are crafted through a writer's imagination, a nonfiction text must contain accurate information that is verifiable by other sources. Nonfiction texts include a variety of organizational aids such as the preface, table of contents, glossary, appendix, and index. Readers who learn to use these features will enhance their comprehension and understanding of informational texts.

- **Preface:** This section is also known as the foreword or introduction. It provides a lead-in for the author(s) to comment on why the book was written and provides clues as to the author's biases. This section will often contain details about the organization of the book and a suggestion about how best to read the book.

- **Table of Contents:** This provides a "road map" of what the book contains by showing how the topics in the book are grouped. It provides an efficient system for finding information that is included under a general topic. Look for texts that are organized in a logical, easy-to-follow manner.

- **Glossary:** This section provides definitions of difficult terms used in the text. It is an essential aid in understanding the vocabulary of a specific subject and a convenient aid for looking up technical and/or difficult terms.

- **Appendix:** An appendix provides additional information about a topic. It is located in the back of the book and contains information that supports and expands a chapter topic. The appendices may also be called a "Student Almanac," "Reference," or "Reference Section."

- **Index:** This section provides the fastest means for locating information on a topic included in the text. It directs the reader to specific pages of the text that address this topic.

Many times students do not need to read an entire nonfiction book to find the information they need. Knowing the parts of a book and their functions will enable students to find information and comprehend meaning more quickly. Spend time previewing the parts of each new text you give students so that they understand how it is organized.

Determine Importance— Using Parts of the Book

Using the Preface

Understanding how to use the preface can motivate students to continue reading. When you guide students through a preview of the book, make sure to spend time skimming and scanning the preface, introduction, and/or foreword. Remind them that a preface is a preliminary statement by the author or editor of the book, setting forth its purpose and scope and sometimes expressing acknowledgment of assistance from others. Allow students opportunities to examine prefaces to see that the acknowledgement section is sometimes separate and quite extensive. Have them think about the following questions as they preview the preface:

- What did the author hope to accomplish in the preface? How do you know?

- How does the information in the preface connect to your prior knowledge on the subject?

- How could the author have improved the preface?

- Am I clear about the general topics and concepts in the book?

- Does the tone and style of the writer connect with my own tone and style?

- Will I enjoy learning this information from this author?

Using the Table of Contents

Reinforce that previewing the table of contents is one of the best tools for self-selecting a book. When students have projects in language arts or research projects across the curriculum, remind them to skim the tables of contents of several books in order to make their selections. Remind them that a table of contents is a list of the sections of the book with page numbers and that these sections may include an introduction, acknowledgments, preface, foreword, chapter titles, appendix, glossary, and index. Some questions to guide students through the previewing process include:

- How does this book or chapter connect to my assigned topic?

- Based on the title, what might I learn about the topic?

- How do these chapter titles connect to what I already know about the topic?

- How do the chapter titles build on each other?

- What will be my cumulative knowledge of the topic after reading this book?

- What chapter titles are missing? What information will I not gain from reading this book?

- Is this book worth my time? Will I achieve my purpose(s) for reading by delving into this book?

Determine Importance— Using Parts of the Book

Using the Glossary

Reinforce that a glossary is essentially a dictionary specific to the nonfiction book they are reading. Students should know that a glossary is a readily available tool for better understanding text information. Motivated and proficient readers will often make the extra effort to seek out a dictionary to define words and terms that they do not understand. However, struggling readers will most likely not make that effort. Remind students that a glossary is a list of words with definitions intended to clarify the basic, technical, dialectical, and/or difficult terms found in the book. The glossary is usually located at the back of the book.

Using the Appendix

When students understand how to use appendices, they can gain additional and substantive information on the topics and concepts presented in the book. Review with students that an appendix is a section of materials that supplements the main text of the book and is usually placed at the end. The appendix includes information that is explanatory or bibliographic such as time lines, graphs, charts, tables, etc. The appendix material is useful, but the book is considered complete without it. Some thought-provoking questions to share with students include:

- How does the information in the appendix add to and extend the facts and concepts that I am studying?

- What practical tips and ideas can I gain from the appendix?

- What statistical information including charts, graphs, and diagrams is included in the appendix? What kind of graphic information should be added?

- What is missing from the appendix? What would I like to know more about?

- What was the author thinking when he or she chose to include _____ in the appendix?

- Is any part of the appendix unnecessary? How so?

- How can I use the information in the appendix to do further research?

Determine Importance—Using Parts of the Book

Using the Index

Remind students that an index is a detailed, alphabetical key to names, places, and topics in a book, including references to their page location(s). Throughout the school year, create opportunities for students to access additional information on the topics being studied by using the index. Allow them to share their thinking as they discover terms that they do not understand, find the different locations for the term, read the different explanations, and determine which explanation best matches the purpose for reading. As a variation, pair each student with a partner and have them share the responsibility for finding the term in multiple locations in the text and determining the best explanation or definition. Students will appreciate the opportunity to discuss the merits of different explanations for a word that they don't understand or about which they need more information.

Using Strategies Independently

Throughout their academic careers, students will need to be able to select nonfiction books by previewing the various parts. Readers should be proficient in using the parts of the book to make good decisions about which books will help them meet their purpose for reading. Provide opportunities for guided practice and make sure that students get opportunities to work in small groups or with a partner to extend their use of previewing strategies. Build their confidence through praise and encouragement when they make wise book selections. Reinforce students' skills by requiring them to justify why they chose the book(s) that they did.

Strategy 1: Previewing the Preface

Have students identify their purpose for reading, allow them to read the preface or introduction, and help them through discussion to understand the author's purpose for writing. Instruct them to use the Previewing the Preface activity (page 190) to identify the background of the book, the major topics to be covered, and the tone. Then they can decide whether they should keep on reading. (Standards 5.1, 5.6)

Strategy 2: Using the Foreword

Once students have identified their purpose for reading, have them complete the Using the Foreword activity (page 191) to identify key words and phrases, to make a prediction about what they will learn, and to explain how the information connects to their prior knowledge and purpose for reading. Then they should ask any further questions that they have about the topic. Emphasize to students that the foreword, preface, and/or introduction all provide critical information to the reader that becomes the foundation for deciding whether to keep reading. (Standards 5.1, 5.6)

Determine Importance—Using Parts of the Book

Strategy 3: Table of Contents Questions

Have students use the activity titled Table of Contents Questions (page 192) to convert each of the chapter titles into a question. Then have them read the chapter and record a general answer to the question. Finally, have students identify at least one additional question they have about the topic in the chapter. The example below shows how students might look at a table of contents and turn each title into a question that they will try to answer as they read. (Standards 5.6, 8.2)

Holiday Traditions Around the World

Table of Contents

Happy New Year! 1

Fun at Carnival 3

The Traditions of Passover 7

Independence Day for America 9

Dia de los Muertos 11

Festival of Lights in Winter 13

Boxing Day. 17

Chapter Titles Converted to Questions

Do all countries celebrate New Year's Day on the same day?

What is Carnival? Which countries celebrate this holiday?

What are the traditions of Passover?

How do we know that July 4th is our Independence Day?

What language is Dia de los Muertos? What does it mean?

What kinds of festivals happen in winter? Do they use a kind of light?

What is Boxing Day and where is it celebrated?

Determine Importance—
Using Parts of the Book

Strategy 4: Using a Glossary

Begin by informing students that some nonfiction books have a built-in dictionary called a glossary. As they read the text, have them identify words with which they are not familiar by recording them on the Using a Glossary activity (page 193). Have students look up the words in the glossary and record the definitions on the chart. Finally, have them reflect on how the definition helps clarify their understanding of the text information. As a variation, have students create an illustrated mini-glossary (page 194). Have students read a short piece of nonfiction text, identify terms with which they are not familiar, use the dictionary to create a short definition, and design a simple illustration or symbol to represent the newly learned word. Using art is always motivating to students and will reinforce their understanding of the glossary. (Standards 5.6, 7.2)

Strategy 5: The Appendix

Guide students in identifying their purpose for reading and allow them to select a nonfiction book to meet that purpose. Provide them with The Appendix activity (page 195) and have them select five topics from the appendix that either match their purpose for reading or simply look interesting. Have them record the topics, page numbers, and definitions or key words in the chart. Allow students to work with a partner to complete this activity. Then have the pairs preview the rest of the book to determine information that might be missing from the appendix. Instruct them to discuss and describe an addition to the appendix that they could create. (Standards 5.6, 7.2)

Strategy 6: Investigating the Index

Lead students to an understanding of their purpose for reading. Then have them use the Investigating the Index activity (page 196) to record unfamiliar words or terms. Instruct students to use the index to locate additional sources of information from throughout the book and record the page numbers on the chart. Finally, after students have investigated each of the identified page numbers, have them reflect on the information that they found most useful. This information can be in the form of facts, details, examples, illustrations, charts, graphs, etc. Allow for the possibility that none of the additional places in the text was useful. Encourage students to discuss the remaining questions they have as well as strategies for finding the information they need. (Standards 5.6, 7.2)

Determine Importance— Using Parts of the Book

Strategy 7: Team Book Investigation

Divide students into groups of four and have them work with their groups to answer the questions on the Team Book Investigation activity (page 197). As students work together, they will be thinking about how the preface, table of contents, index, and appendix help them achieve their purpose for reading. Have them examine different books and communicate their findings to the class. (Standards 5.6, 7.2)

Strategy 8: Evaluating the Parts of a Nonfiction Book

Take students to the school library to select a nonfiction book or have them choose one from the classroom library. Make sure to identify the purpose for reading or guide students in identifying their own purposes for reading. Provide them with the activity titled Evaluating the Parts of a Nonfiction Book (page 198). Have them record the parts of the book and make observations about the content of the book by commenting on facts, details, length, attractiveness, and author's purpose. Finally, have them evaluate the usefulness of each part of the book by reflecting on their purposes for reading. (Standards 5.6, 7.2)

Strategy 9: Text Coding

Marking the text is a great monitoring tool for students to use in order to ensure that they are meeting their purposes for reading. Present students with three codes: **C** to represent the concept they are studying; **M** to represent what further information they need; and **?** to represent the information that they do not understand. If possible, instruct them to mark directly in the text; otherwise, use sticky notes or create a bookmark on which to record the codes. When they are finished reading and marking text, have them record the corresponding text information on the Text Coding activity (page 199). Then have them identify the part of the book that they think will be the most useful in finding more information or clarifying their confusion. Finally, instruct students to identify the information that they found. (Standards 7.3, 7.5)

Text Coding

Determine Importance— Using Parts of the Book

Strategy 10: Analyzing the Author's Choices

Being critical of the author's choices is an important skill that proficient readers possess. Have students use the Analyzing the Author's Choices activity (page 200) to identify the major components of a nonfiction book. Then have them evaluate the author by deciding through careful examination whether each of these parts is comprehensive, attractive, helpful, interesting, organized, and connected to the main idea(s) of the book. Encourage students to elaborate using adequate examples and to offer suggestions about the revisions that the author should make. You may need to model this evaluation for students depending on their maturity and skill levels. (Standards 5.1, 5.5)

Strategy 11: Locating Information with a Partner

Students can use the Locating Information with a Partner activity (page 201) to work in pairs to find information in various parts of a book. The pairs can determine a topic of study and then determine the best place in the book to find the needed information. (Standards 5.6, 7.2)

Determine Importance— Using Parts of the Book

Previewing the Preface

Directions: Analyze the preface of a nonfiction book.

Definition of the preface: a preliminary statement by the author or editor of a book that sets forth its purpose and scope and/or expresses acknowledgment of assistance from others

Purpose for reading: _____

Author's purpose: _____

Description of the background of the book (may include where the idea of the book came from):

_____

_____

_____

_____

_____

_____

_____

What are the major topics covered in the book (scope)? _____

_____

_____

_____

What is the tone of the book (formal/informal; informative/entertaining; chatty/serious, etc.)? Explain.

_____

_____

_____

Will you keep reading based on the preface? Explain._____

_____

_____

_____

Determine Importance—
Using Parts of the Book

Using the Foreword

Directions: Analyze the foreword of a nonfiction text.

Definition of the foreword: an introduction or preface to the book

Purpose for reading: _____

_____

What are the key words or phrases from the foreword?	What do you predict that you will learn?
How will this information connect to your prior knowledge and/or your purpose for reading?	What questions do you have about the topic based on the foreword?

Determine Importance— Using Parts of the Book

Table of Contents Questions

Directions: Change the chapter titles to questions, record a general answer, and generate a new question about the contents of the chapter.

Definition of the table of contents: a list of the sections of the book with page numbers (sections include: introduction, acknowledgments, preface, foreword, chapter titles, appendix, glossary, index, etc.)

Chapter title	Convert chapter title to a question	General answer	A new question

Determine Importance— Using Parts of the Book

Using a Glossary

Directions: As you read, record words with which you are unfamiliar. Look up these words in the glossary and record the definition in your own words. Then identify how the definition helped you clarify the text information.

Definition of a glossary: a list of words with definitions intended to clarify the basic, technical, dialectical, and/or difficult terms found in the book

Terms/words with which you are unfamiliar	Definition in your own words	How does this definition help clarify your understanding of the text information? How does this definition connect to what you are learning in the classroom?

Determine Importance— Using Parts of the Book

Creating an Illustrated Mini-Glossary

Directions: Create an illustrated mini-glossary that will help the reader understand the text information. As you read, highlight or underline words that you do not understand. Then record the words below, look them up in a dictionary and restate the definition in a simpler way in your own words. Finally, create an illustration or symbol to represent the word.

Term/word	Brief definition	Illustration/symbol

Determine Importance—
Using Parts of the Book

The Appendix

Directions: Identify your purpose for reading, select a nonfiction book, and then preview the appendix. Select five topics that match your purpose. Record the topics and the page numbers in the chart. Then look up each topic and record the definition or key words and phrases about the topic.

Definition of an appendix: A section of materials that supplements the main text of the book and is usually placed at the end. The appendix includes examples of various portions of the text and other information that is explanatory or bibliographic. The appendix material is useful, but the book is considered complete without it.

Purpose for reading: _____

_____

Topic	Page number	Definition or key words and phrases from the text that describe the topic

Determine Importance—
Using Parts of the Book

Investigating the Index

Directions: Identify your purpose for reading. As you read, record unfamiliar words or terms. Use the index to locate additional sources of information. Record the facts, details, and examples in the book that best helped you understand the unfamiliar word or term and achieve your purpose for reading.

Definition of an index: a detailed alphabetical key to names, places, and topics in a book including references to their page location(s)

Purpose for reading: _____

_____

Unfamiliar word or term	Page numbers where additional information can be found	Information that is most useful (details, facts, examples) or further questions about the term

Determine Importance—Using Parts of the Book

Team Book Investigation

Directions: In your group of four, assign each member a question to answer. Record your answers in the boxes below.

Purpose for reading: _____

_____

What information from the preface will help us achieve our purpose?	How will the table of contents help us achieve our purpose?
What information from the appendix will be helpful?	How will the index help us achieve our purpose?

Determine Importance—
Using Parts of the Book

Evaluating the Parts of a Nonfiction Book

Directions: Begin by identifying your purpose for reading. Then identify the parts of the nonfiction book you have chosen, make observations about the content, and evaluate the usefulness of that part. Use the usefulness ratings below to make your prediction.

Possible parts of a nonfiction book: preface, foreword, introduction, acknowledgments, table of contents, chapters, index, glossary, and appendix

Purpose for reading: _____

_____

Usefulness ratings:

- Highly useful   • Somewhat useful   • Not very useful

Part of the book	Observations about content (facts, details, length, attractiveness, author's purpose, etc.)	Prediction about usefulness in terms of meeting your purpose

Determine Importance— Using Parts of the Book

Text Coding

Directions: As you are reading, use the codes below to mark the text. If you cannot write on the text, use sticky notes, or make a little bookmark to line up with the text and mark your codes. When you are finished, fill in the chart below. Record the text information that you found in the left column and the section(s) of the nonfiction book that you think will help you the most in the center column. Finally, use the right column to record the information that you found.

C = How does this idea **connect** to the concept I am studying?

M = I'd like to know **more** about this topic.

? = **I don't understand** this information.

Possible parts of a nonfiction book: preface, foreword, introduction, acknowledgments, table of contents, chapters, index, glossary, appendix

Text information (what you want to know more about or your question regarding the information you don't understand)	Section of the book you think will be most useful	What you found

Determine Importance— Using Parts of the Book

Analyzing the Author's Choices

Directions: Evaluate the contents of each of the parts of the nonfiction book identified on the left.

Part of the nonfiction book	Analysis: Is this part comprehensive? Attractive? Helpful? Interesting? Connected to the main idea of the book? Organized? Explain your answer fully. Be sure to offer suggestions about what the author could improve, add, change, or delete.
Preface, foreword, or introduction	
Table of contents	
Glossary	
Appendix	
Index	

Determine Importance—
Using Parts of the Book

Locating Information with a Partner

Directions: Locate information in a nonfiction text with a partner.

Possible parts of a nonfiction book: preface, foreword, introduction, acknowledgments, table of contents, chapters, index, glossary, appendix

Topic: _____

What questions do we have about the topic? What do we want to know more about?	What information did we find to answer our questions? What further questions do we have?
Did the author do a good job including necessary parts of the book in order to assist the reader?	Which part of the book was most useful in finding answers to our questions?

Notes

Visualize

PASSPORT TO COMPREHENSION

#50470 Successful Strategies

Visualize

Introduction

Strategic readers visualize both during and after reading. These visual images include all the senses, as well as emotions based on the reader's prior knowledge and experiences. These visualizations help readers immerse themselves in the reading, making the details richer and more memorable. Visualizations can be used to draw conclusions, make inferences, and recall important details. Visual images are revised and adapted as the reading continues and new information is uncovered. After sharing visualizations with other readers, the strategic reader will modify and adjust his or her own previous impressions, incorporating the different viewpoints. All of these factors contribute to increased comprehension.

Closely related to inferring, visualizing requires the reader to make "mind movies," pictures, and sensory impressions based on what has been read. Visualizing strengthens higher-level, divergent thinking. It asks the reader to draw on past experiences and impressions and weave them into the written text. This technique enables the reader to become more intimately involved with the text and derive deeper meaning. Many studies have demonstrated that when students use visualization strategies, they are able to comprehend and recall key ideas more effectively. When making abstract concepts more concrete through visualization, students retain the information better.

By teaching students to use visualization and imagery techniques, teachers help students learn more effectively. Students also acquire a strategy that will help them assume control of their own learning in the future.

Although visualization is more commonly used in fictional texts, these strategies can be applied to nonfiction texts as well. Using visualization in science can assist students in learning and retaining complicated concepts, such as cell structure and function and photosynthesis, and mechanical concepts, such as force, speed, and work. In math, visualization can be used to give students a frame of reference when comparing different measurements, such as gram, kilogram, hectogram, and so on. Social studies is an area where visualization can enrich otherwise dry historical facts and motivate students to learn more about a particular period in history.

Visualize

Inferring through Visualization

Visualizing is one of the mental building blocks for proficiency in making inferences. Teachers need to be aware that students can use words from text, titles, charts, diagrams, and illustrations to make inferences and thus improve their abilities to understand the information. An effective approach to presenting the idea of inferring is to share some specific descriptions or scenarios and have students make an inference about the events in the scenario. For example, a seventh-grade boy comes home from a baseball game with a smile on his face. His family can infer that he either won the game or made a very good play offensively or defensively. After presenting students with many such scenarios, their confidence with inferring will improve.

Next, you can move on to inferring with text. Share with students some descriptive scenarios from the text that create a visual picture in their minds. For example, the author describes a scene where the main character is shopping in the mall. The teacher can lead the students to see many stores, an escalator or elevators, and other shoppers. Filling in the missing information will help students comprehend textual information.

Tapping into Prior Knowledge

Guided practice with previewing text will help students tap into their prior knowledge. Before students begin reading, have them look carefully at the title and identify any visual images associated with the words. Then have them preview the text, noting the headings, subheadings, charts, graphs, and illustrations and identify visual images associated with these various text features. It may help to record these observations on the board. Finally, have students make connections between these visual images and their prior knowledge of the topic. As they read, refer them to their initial visualizations and ask them to revise or clarify their understandings.

Sensory Detail

Proficient readers use sensory details to make pictures in their minds. These readers see, hear, taste, touch, and smell the images that are described in the text. Teachers need to model how to create pictures in one's mind when reading. Proficient readers create mental images but often don't realize what is going on cognitively in order for them to "see" the text. Teachers must help these readers understand the visualizing skills that they have developed in order to build on these skills and, additionally, help struggling readers use sensory details to begin the process of visualizing text.

Visualize

Creating Mental Images to Remember Details

Retention is a critical component of reading comprehension. As proficient readers enter the text and begin to form vague pictures of the big ideas, they will also begin to add distinctive impressions of the details. As educators, we often ask students to simply retain the facts, details, and small ideas. It is important to teach students that building a strong ability to visualize will help them retain the big idea(s) and provide the scaffolding on which to hang the details. When we assess students' progress, it is valuable to incorporate many kinds of evaluation. A unit test may include some multiple choice, true/false, short-answer, and long-answer responses. In addition to the traditional approaches to assessment, include a question that asks students to reflect upon how they used visualization to remember key concepts, facts, and details. Such a component of assessment will help them build their metacognitive abilities and ultimately strengthen their retention of information.

Creating Mental Images to Draw Conclusions

Drawing conclusions is a skill essential in all subject areas. When students are able to visualize text information, they are better able to understand the relationships among ideas and draw conclusions about the information that they are learning. One strategy that is very useful in helping students with this skill is providing them with a "purpose for reading" question that requires them to think about the conclusions that they are drawing as they read. Be sure to have them identify the specific text information that allowed them to draw their conclusions.

Incorporating New Information

One of the key features of learning and teaching is the fact that new information builds on what is already known. If students gain proficiency in linking new information to what they already know about the topic and making connections across contexts and subject areas, then their learning will improve exponentially. The questions on the following page can be used to ask students to help them build their visualizing skills and make connections in order to incorporate new information into their existing knowledge base.

Visualize

Incorporating New Information (cont.)

Questions for Visualizing Text

Before Reading

- What do you already know about the topic?

- As you preview the text, what images do you see?

- What images do you already have that are related to your current knowledge or understanding of the topic?

- Can you describe these images?

- Can you represent these images either through art or drama?

During Reading

- What new information are you learning about the topic?

- What images do you associate with this new information?

- Are you visualizing as you read?

- Can you describe these images?

- How do these new images confirm or contradict the images that you identified before you began reading?

After Reading

- What key information (concepts, topics, facts) did you learn?

- Have you blended your existing images about the topic with your new images?

- Can you represent the connections you have made between your existing knowledge and new knowledge through art, drama, or writing?

- How does visualizing improve the learning process?

- What strategies did you use to visualize the information you were learning?

- How can you apply these strategies in other content areas?

Other questions to help students visualize text are provided on page 219.

Visualize

Representing Abstract Information as Mental Pictures

One of the most difficult skills is representing abstract information as a mental picture. For example, if a teacher asks students to read about freedom, he or she may ask them first to identify pictures that come to mind, such as the American flag, the bald eagle, or the Statue of Liberty. As students read, they should be instructed to add to their mental pictures by using information from the text.

Using Strategies Independently

What follows is a list of strategies designed to improve students' visualization abilities when reading. Make sure to model how to visualize through think alouds and talk alouds in which you share with students the images you create in your mind as you read and your thinking as you try to make sense of the text. Demonstrate for students how to use each strategy on the board and/or overhead. Most importantly, share your enthusiasm for reading and the confusion and misconceptions that you encounter when reading. Gradually release the responsibility for using strategies to students by observing carefully their proficiencies and confidence levels with each new strategy you present.

Strategy 1: Double-Entry Journal

Double-entry journals are a very effective tool for building students' metacognitive skills. When working on visualizing, instruct students to read carefully for images and use the double-entry journal (page 220) to record sensory images on the left side. Then have students draw a picture or describe the images in their heads on the right side. Double-entry journals focusing on abstract-concept development (page 221) add an extra dimension to the reading process. (Standards 5.4, 7.4)

Strategy 2: Text Coding and Visualizing

Having students code text helps them increase their comprehension during reading. Begin by refreshing their memories about the five senses. Share with them the five codes to use for identifying images that appeal to the five senses (an eye for sight, a nose for smell, an ear for sound, a tongue for taste, a hand for touch). Find a short piece of descriptive text, and make an overhead transparency. With an overhead marker, use the appropriate code to mark words, phrases, or sentences that appeal to particular senses. Share the coding activity (page 222) with students. Instruct them to read a piece of text, code for sensory detail and then use the activity to respond to the sensory images that they identified. (Standards 5.4, 7.4)

Visualize

Strategy 3: Listening to Music

Using music is an effective strategy when introducing the skill of visualizing. Classical music, such as the *William Tell Overture* or excerpts from Tchaikovsky's *Nutcracker Suite*, will evoke many images in students' minds. Begin by giving them the guide for Listening to Music (page 223) and instructing them to record as many images as possible as they listen to the music. You may need to demonstrate this procedure with a short piece of music. For example, a fast-paced selection of music with a lively rhythm might evoke the image of cowboys riding their horses on the open prairie or fairies dancing in the woods and playing hide-and-seek. After students finish listening to the music and recording their images, have them use the right side of the listening guide to write a brief story, poem, or description that incorporates the images. Emphasize to students that they need to apply the ability to visualize while listening to music to their reading. (Standards 5.4, 7.4)

Strategy 4: Text Graphing

Text graphing allows students to visualize the information they are learning as well as evaluate it. This technique is particularly effective in social studies classes. Have students list the events that they are encountering in the text. Next, have them think of an artistic representation or symbol for each of the events. Present them with the Text Graphing activity (page 224). Have them evaluate each of the events as a "positive event" or a "negative event" based on the feeling it elicits. It is important to note that there are not any right or wrong answers in text graphing and that different students may rate events differently. For example, the Americans' defeat of the British at the Battle of Yorktown might be evaluated as a +4 because of the Americans' victory but not receive a +5 rating because many lives were lost in the process. After students have evaluated the events, they can mark the events by drawing the symbol for that event next to its corresponding number on the graph. Students should be encouraged to justify their ratings either in writing or in small-group or whole-group discussions. (Standards 5.4, 7.4)

Visualize

Strategy 5: Parts-of-Speech Visualizing

This simple technique reinforces parts of speech and requires students to categorize the images they are encountering. Present them with the Parts-of-Speech Visualizing organizer (page 225) and have them record specific nouns, vivid verbs, interesting adjectives and adverbs, and prepositional phrases as they read. After completing this section of the activity, students evaluate the author's word choice. (Standards 5.3, 5.4)

Strategy 6: Predicting and Inferring Chart

Predicting, inferring, and visualizing are skills that overlap in the repertoire of essential proficiencies that good readers must have. Have students read and record images in the left column of the Predicting and Inferring Chart (page 226). After they record these images, have them make predictions about what will happen next. Finally, instruct them to draw inferences based on the images and predictions they have made. Guide them toward inferences that connect to the larger concepts they are studying. This technique works particularly well with social studies and science concepts and topics. (Standards 7.3, 7.4)

Strategy 7: Rotating Dramas

Pair students with a partner and instruct each to take on the role of a different character from the text. Then have them interact with each other through dialogue or movement. This interaction should take no longer than a minute or two and will create a vivid image in students' minds regarding the relationships between the people, ideas, or concepts in their reading. This technique works across all content areas. For example, the characters in social studies may be historical figures or people who live in other countries; the characters in science may be chemicals, elements, or scientific concepts; the characters in math may be numbers, signs, or symbols. The pairs should present their dramas to the class. (Standards 7.3, 7.4)

Strategy 8: Tableaus

A tableau is a frozen scene from the text and is a nonthreatening way to get every student in the class interacting with a text. Students need to work with partners or in groups to create their tableaus. Assign each group a different portion of the text to dramatize. Students work cooperatively to create a frozen scene that depicts the relationship between people, ideas, or concepts from the text. There is no dialogue in a tableau, although students may choose to have their characters engage in a repetitive movement to show some particular feature of the idea or concept they are dramatizing. After students have created their tableaus, they should perform them in front of the class. A variation of this strategy has the class guessing which part of the text they are dramatizing. (Standards 7.3, 7.4)

Visualize

Strategy 9: Mini-Drama

Mini-dramas allow students in teams or pairs to summarize what they have learned in an interactive way. Have them use the Mini-Drama planning sheets (pages 227 and 228) to identify characters, concepts, and facts that they will incorporate into their mini-dramas. Then instruct them to plan a brief dialogue that demonstrates the relationship(s) between ideas. Mini-dramas are a great technique to help students build their visualization skills. The teams or pairs present their dramas to the class. (Standards 7.3, 7.4)

Strategy 10: Talk Show

Planning a talk show will get students involved in writing dialogues, developing opinions, and interviewing characters in order to demonstrate their knowledge of a particular concept or idea. Have them use the activity on page 229 to plan their talk show in cooperative groups. These groups will then present their talk shows to the class. (Standards 7.3, 7.4)

Strategy 11: Symbolic Story Representations

Symbolic story representations involve a technique in which students are given pieces of differently colored construction paper and use the paper to tear shapes that represent different ideas, concepts, or characters from the text (Enciso 1992). Then they arrange the shapes on a large piece of construction paper in order to show the relationships between or among the ideas. Finally, students explain their creations in small groups or through a written response. The simple act of tearing shapes is highly motivating and is a nonthreatening way for them to represent their ideas since little to no artistic ability is required. (Standards 7.3, 7.4)

Strategy 12: Storyboarding

An essential step in the planning process of movies and TV shows, storyboarding is also a great way for students to visualize the sequence of steps in a scientific experiment or the events that unfolded during a particular time in history. Introduce the idea of storyboarding to students by showing them the Storyboarding activity (page 230) and having them think about a sequence of events or steps with which they are familiar. For example, they can think of their morning routine before coming to school. Then have students read the text and illustrate through symbols and simple illustrations the sequence or steps in the text. Students may work in small groups or pairs and present their storyboards to the class. (Standards 7.3, 7.4)

Visualize

Strategy 13: Differentiated Instruction

Students thrive on differentiated instruction. Create different corners of the classroom that are dedicated to different learning styles. One corner of the classroom could be called the "Dramatic Dugout." In this corner, provide space for three to four performers and three to four audience members. The Dramatic Dugout should have multiple texts, dramatic scenarios, and supplies for making scenery and props. Another corner could be called "Discussion Detour." In this corner, provide for four to six students to engage in a discussion about the texts they are reading. This corner should have multiple texts, discussion frames, and sentence starters, as well as a tape recorder so that students can tape their discussions and reflect on their communication skills. A third corner could be titled the "Artist's Arena" and should provide a rich supply of art materials for students to create representations of the texts they are reading. The final corner could be titled "Writer's Retreat" and should include space and supplies for four to eight writers to reflect on their reading or create their own text representing key ideas and concepts they are learning. (Standards 5.4, 7.3)

Strategy 14: Making a Postcard

Having students visualize various audiences helps them strengthen their reading skills. Instruct them to use pages 231 and 232 to create a postcard that demonstrates a relationship between characters or ideas in the text. Students will have to use their inferring skills to conceive of such an interaction and use their visualization skills to imagine the sender, receiver, and location that the postcard depicts. In social studies, examples include the creation of postcards between historical figures. In science, examples include postcards that show the interaction between neutrons and protons, veins and arteries, or animals that occupy the same habitat. This activity can also be done by providing students with 4" x 6" (10 cm x 15 cm) blank index cards. On one side students write the message and address, and on the other side they can draw a picture representing the subject, event, or place. (Standards 5.4, 7.3)

Strategy 15: Using Poetry to Create Movies in the Mind

Poetry is an excellent method for activating visualization. (Standards 5.4, 7.3)

A guided visualization session with students might go something like this:

Teacher: Before we get started, I want you to get into a comfortable position at your desks. I want you to sit straight but relaxed with your hands folded in front of you on your desk. Take a deep breath through your nose, and then slowly let it out through your mouth. Let's do that a few times. Slowly inhale through the nose; exhale through the mouth. I'm going to read something to you now, and I want you to listen carefully. As you are listening with your eyes closed, I want you to picture in your mind what is happening. Be sure to think not only about how things look, but also how they sound, feel, smell. Think about the emotions you are feeling as you visualize the events as they unfold.

The teacher then reads the poem "Zephyr Queen" by Ilyse McKennaugh (page 233) without commentary or interpretation.

Teacher: I'm going to re-read parts of this poem, and I want you to imagine that you are watching a movie about what is happening. Close your eyes and picture in your mind a movie that shows what is going on.

Visualize

Strategy 15: Using Poetry to Create Movies in the Mind *(cont.)*

Teacher reads:

> *It was one of those rare summer days,*
>
> *When it wasn't too hot,*
>
> *Nor too steamy.*
>
> *The air was pure and fresh,*
>
> *As I lay on the dewy grass,*
>
> *Green and sweet-smelling.*
>
> *And I watched.*
>
> *The sky above went up into forever,*
>
> *While breezes brushed my hair,*
>
> *And the sun's rays caressed my face,*
>
> *And the world was clean and new.*

Teacher: Who would like to describe the movie they are seeing?

Student #1: It makes me think about my dad and I going hunting.

Student #2: I see our vacation last year when we went to Yosemite National Park. It was so green there!

Teacher: Those are some good mind movies! Does anyone see himself or herself in the movie?

Student #3: Yeah! I see myself walking down a dirt road behind my grandma's house. She lives out in the country.

Teacher: You bring up a good point. Everyone who has shared his or her mind movies has described something that is out in the country, out in nature. What words made you think it was out in the country?

Student #4: When you said the sky was high and the grass was green and everything was so clean, it made me think of being out in the woods.

Teacher: Good observation. Now I want all of you to close your eyes again and in your minds, go back to that movie you started. Listen to the next part:

> *Cotton candy clouds were fantasy creatures*
>
> *From a long-ago time when knights battled dragons*
>
> *For the hands of their Ladies.*
>
> *A floating scrap of black velvet caught my eye.*

Visualize

Strategy 15: Using Poetry to Create Movies in the Mind *(cont.)*

High above the earth,

Floating downward,

Ever closer.

I recognized her regal form.

Her wings conveying her without effort,

Like Cleopatra on the royal barge,

Floating on a Nile of clouds.

Teacher: Has anyone added something to his or her mind movies?

Student #5: Yeah! When you said there was something black floating in the sky, I started thinking about a big, black bird. Maybe a crow or something.

Student #6: Me too! I saw a bird in my movie, but to me it was a hawk.

Student #7: You guys are both wrong! It was an eagle; they have white heads.

Student #6: How do you know it had a white head? I don't remember hearing that! Are you sure?

Teacher: You all have good ideas—let's read on to find out what kind of bird it really is. I'm gong to read some more, and I want you to close your eyes again, and add to the movie you have started in your mind. Remember, it's perfectly fine to change some of the details in your movie.

Teacher reads:

And the sun's rays caressed my face,

And the world was clean and new.

As I watched her solitary passage,

The sun flashed

On her Crown of white feathers.

She wheeled ever nearer,

Her keen gaze never faltering from her prey,

When a cloud monster surrounded her,

Snatched her up in its claws.

And the sun's rays caressed my face,

And the world was clean and new.

Teacher: What have you added to your mind movie?

Student #5: I've changed my mind—it isn't a crow. I think it *is* an eagle!

Strategy 15: Using Poetry to Create Movies in the Mind *(cont.)*

Teacher: What made you change your mind?

Student #5: When you said the part about the bird having white on his head. Crows are all black, but eagles have white on their heads.

Teacher: Great attention to details. It is okay to change your opinion when you have more facts. Anything else?

Student #7: Well, I pictured the bird getting lost in the clouds. Then I couldn't see it anymore.

Teacher: What was it that made you think it was lost in the clouds?

Student #7: The part about the cloud that was shaped like a monster grabbing the bird. I know it didn't really eat the bird; it was just my imagination because the cloud looked like a monster.

Teacher: Excellent interpretation of a metaphor! When the author says, "a cloud monster," she doesn't mean a real dragon, does she? I'm glad you picked up on that. Now let's add some more to our mind movies:

> *Shielding my eyes,*
>
> *I watched,*
>
> *I waited,*
>
> *Then I saw her.*
>
> *Again a scrap of black velvet*
>
> *As she escaped the cloud monster.*
>
> *Becoming ever smaller,*
>
> *Farther away.*
>
> *Then she was gone.*

Student #8: I see the eagle coming out of the clouds, but now it's farther away!

Teacher: Let's listen to the last part and add it to your mind movie:

> *And on days when the snow drifts high*
>
> *Outside my window,*
>
> *I sit by the fire,*
>
> *Recalling the Zephyr Queen.*
>
> *And I remember that*
>
> *The sun's rays caressed my face,*
>
> *And the world was clean and new.*

Visualize

Strategy 15: Using Poetry to Create Movies in the Mind *(cont.)*

Student #8: Yeah, it's an eagle. The rest of you weren't listening.

Teacher: You have a good memory, but it's all right when people need to read or hear something again so that they can visualize what's going on. If I told you the word "zephyr" means a soft and gentle wind, what does that tell you about the subject of the poem?

Student #5: It makes me imagine an eagle even more because they fly and glide so smoothly. So an eagle would be a king or a queen of the winds and the air.

Teacher: Good interpretation. Now, would anyone like to share with us his or her entire movie?

Student #3: Well, I'm walking along the dirt road behind my grandma's house. She lives on a farm and there are a lot of wild animals around. Sometimes we see deer and raccoons and stuff. I'm walking along and I look up into the sky and I see this huge eagle! I'm excited about it because I've never seen a wild eagle before. I stop and watch it fly; it's so bright that I have to shade my eyes from the sun. The eagle flies and soars in the sky—it looks like my remote-control plane—and then it flies into some clouds; and I don't see it anymore. I keep watching, though, and before long, it comes out of the clouds. Now it's farther away, and I guess it's flying back to its nest somewhere. Maybe it's hunting for food for baby eagles. Hey—does the father eagle take care of the babies, or just the mother? Anyway, I watch it until I can't see it anymore; then I run back to my grandma's. I can't wait to tell her and Grandpa about it.

Teacher: That's a very rich mind movie! So many details. Thanks for sharing that with us. It was interesting to me that you mentioned that you had never seen a wild eagle before. I never have either. The only place I have ever seen a live eagle is at the zoo. I read somewhere that very few people ever get to see wild eagles. Does anyone know why?

At this point, the teacher can launch into a science lesson about endangered species, the use of pesticides, wildlife conservation, etc. This is a great way not only to help students visualize concepts that they are learning, but also to activate prior knowledge and set a purpose for learning. An activity like this one helps engage students' imaginations and gets them talking about their thoughts.

When choosing poems that deal with content-area subjects, look for those that have simple language and evoke strong images.

Visualize

Strategy 15: Using Poetry to Create Movies in the Mind *(cont.)*

Other content-area poems suitable for visualization practice include:

"Paul Revere's Ride" by Henry Wadsworth Longfellow (social studies)

"Oh Captain! My Captain!" by Walt Whitman (social studies)

"I, Too" by Langston Hughes (social studies)

"Concord Hymn" by Ralph Waldo Emerson (social studies)

"The New Colossus" by Emma Lazarus (social studies)

"A Country Boy in Winter" by Sarah Orne Jewett (science & nature)

"Dawn" by William Carlos Williams (science & nature)

"The Great Figure" by William Carlos Williams (fire safety)

"The Tulip Bed" by William Carlos Williams (science & nature)

"The Snowing of the Pines" by Thomas Wentworth Higginson (science & nature)

"The West Wind" by John Masefield (science & nature)

"Bagley Wood" by Lionel Johnson (science & nature)

"A Child's Garden of Verses" by Robert Louis Stevenson (science & nature)

"Helen Keller" by Edmund Clarence Stedman (social studies)

"Landing of the Pilgrims" by Felicia Dorothea Hermans (social studies)

"The Cloud" by Percy Bysshe Shelley (science & nature)

"Afternoon on a Hill" by Edna St. Vincent Millay (science & nature)

"Heat" by Hilda Doolittle (science & nature)

"The Rain" by W.H. Davies (science & nature)

"Never and Forever" by George Charles Selden (science & nature)

"The Twelve Months" by George Ellis (seasons)

"October" by Paul Laurence Dunbar (seasons)

"Fog" by Carl Sandburg (weather)

Whenever using poetry for visualization and activation of prior knowledge, always remember to bring the lesson back to the moment and relate what has been discussed to the topic at hand. This strategy will facilitate the bridging of knowledge from one area to another.

Visualize

Questions for Visualizing Text

Directions: Use the following questions to help you visualize the text.

What pictures are you forming in your mind of people, places, things, and ideas?

What details from the text are helping you create a picture in your mind?

What details from your own experience are you adding to the picture in your own mind?

If you were to make a movie using the pictures in your mind, what would you use for background music?

If you were to make a movie using the pictures in your mind, what colors and shading would you use to represent mood?

Are you seeing in your mind what the author intended you to see? Why do you think so?

How would you describe the pictures or images in your mind to a friend?

Do you see yourself interacting with the people, places, things, or ideas that you are visualizing in your mind? Explain.

What images or details are missing from the text? Can you fill in these images in your own mind?

Do the images, based on text information, that you see in your mind remind you of a personal memory? Explain.

Do the images and ideas in your mind remind you of other texts that you have read on the same topic? Explain.

What if a major idea in the text were deleted? How would this deletion change the pictures in your mind?

If you were to paint a picture of a major idea from the text, what would it look like? What colors and textures would you use?

Imagine a dialogue between people or ideas in the text. What are the contents of the dialogue and the voice tones of the people/ideas?

How does visualizing ideas from the text help you make inferences?

Visualize

Double-Entry Journal—Visualization

Directions: As you read, record a passage that includes many sensory details and then either draw or describe the image that is in your head. In the first column, quote or list sensory details from the text. Then provide a drawing of what is in your head or a description that includes details that are not in the text.

Details	Illustrations

Visualize

Double-Entry Journal—Visualizing Abstract Information

Directions: As you read, record information about the concept or topic that you are studying. Use a quote or words that represent the concept or idea in the text. Then draw a picture of what you see in your mind as you read.

Quote or words	Illustration

My response: This image reminds me of…

_____

_____

_____

_____

_____

_____

_____

_____

_____

_____

Visualize

Text Coding and Visualizing

Directions: As you read, use the following codes to mark in the margins or on a sticky note next to significant segments of text. Then use the chart below to record your answers to the questions for quality visualizing.

- Picture of an eye—details that appeal to sight
- Picture of a nose—details that appeal to smell
- Picture of an ear—details that appeal to sound
- Picture of a tongue—details that appeal to taste
- Picture of a hand—details that appeal to touch

Details from the text (Use the text coding to find text information.)	**Response** (Choose from the sentence starters below to get you started on your response.) • This image reminds me of… • The details from my own mind that I added to the text information include… • The author included these details in order to… • I wonder…

Visualize

Listening to Music

Directions: As you listen to the music, record as many images as you can in the left side of the chart. When the music is finished, use the right side to write a response to the music using the images. This response can be in the form of a creative short story, a poem, or a description of a memory. Be creative and descriptive.

Images from the music	Response (short story, poem, description of a memory, etc.)

Visualize

Text Graphing

Directions: Using events from the text, illustrate positive events in the top half of the chart and negative events in the bottom half of the chart. Use the +5 to -5 rating system to indicate the degree of positive or negative feelings associated with the event. The center horizontal line is "0."

+5

+4

+3

+2

+1

-1

-2

-3

-4

-5

Visualize

Parts-of-Speech Visualizing

Directions: As you are reading, record specific nouns, vivid verbs, interesting adjectives or adverbs, and helpful prepositional phrases.

Specific nouns	Vivid verbs
Interesting adjectives and adverbs	**Prepositional phrases**

Do you think the author did a good job of creating a picture in your mind by using different parts of speech? Explain.

_____

_____

_____

_____

_____

Visualize

Predicting and Inferring Chart

Directions: Record key images from the text. Then make predictions and inferences by using the guiding questions provided for you.

Images from the text	Predictions: What will the author include next about the topic?

Inferring: How does the text information connect to the major concept you are studying?

_____

_____

_____

_____

_____

_____

_____

_____

Visualize

Mini-Drama

Directions: With your team member(s), plan out a mini-drama that shows what you have learned.

Student names	Characters	Main character traits

Key concept(s) you will dramatize: _____

_____

_____

Facts from your learning: _____

_____

_____

_____

_____

_____

_____

_____

_____

_____

_____

_____

Visualize

Mini-Drama *(cont.)*

Create a dialogue that shows key concepts, facts learned, and relationships among ideas. (Use the back of this page if you need more space.)

_____

_____

_____

_____

_____

_____

_____

_____

_____

_____

_____

_____

_____

_____

_____

_____

_____

_____

_____

_____

_____

_____

_____

_____

_____

_____

_____

_____

_____

_____

_____

Visualize

Talk Show

Directions: With your team, plan a talk show that shows the knowledge you have gained about the topic or concept you are studying.

Student names	Talk show host(s)	Talk show guest(s)

Visual aids that will be used in the talk show to illustrate the topics learned:

_____

_____

_____

Each of the talk show participants will have to plan a talk show that includes information about the topic(s) in the text. Each member will need to use separate lined notebook paper to plan and write the talk show. Use the following questions to guide you:

1. Who are the main characters in the talk show? (historical figures in social studies; chemicals or elements in science; signs or symbols in mathematics)

2. What is their interaction? What is the problem?

3. When did this interaction or problem occur?

4. Where did the important information take place?

5. Why is the information important?

6. What is the overall message that the talk show host wants the audience to learn?

Visualize

Storyboarding

Directions: Illustrate the events, process, or steps as they occurred in the text.

Event #1	Event #2	Event #3
Event #4	**Event #5**	**Event #6**
Event #7	**Event #8**	**Event #9**
Event #10	**Event #11**	**Event #12**

Visualize

Making a Postcard

Directions: Create a postcard that is sent from one person or idea in the text to another person or idea. Use the front of the card (below) to draw the location from which the postcard is sent. Use the back of the card (page 232) to describe the location, write a message, draw an appropriate stamp, and write the address to which it is being sent.

Front of Postcard

Visualize

Making a Postcard *(cont.)*

Back of Postcard

Description of setting

(Message)

_____

_____

_____

_____

_____

_____

_____

_____

_____

(Stamp)

(Address)

_____

_____

_____

Visualize

Zephyr Queen
by Ilyse McKennaugh

It was one of those rare summer days,
When it wasn't too hot,
Nor too steamy.
The air was pure and fresh,
As I lay on the dewy grass,
Green and sweet-smelling.
And I watched.
The sky above went up into forever,
While breezes brushed my hair,
And the sun's rays caressed my face,
And the world was clean and new.

Cotton candy clouds were fantasy
creatures
From a long-ago time when knights
battled dragons
For the hands of their Ladies.
A floating scrap of black velvet caught my
eye.
High above the earth,
Floating downward,
Ever closer.
I recognized her regal form.
Her wings conveying her without effort,
Like Cleopatra on the royal barge,
Floating on a Nile of clouds.
And the sun's rays caressed my face,
And the world was clean and new.

As I watched her solitary passage,
The sun flashed
On her Crown of white feathers.
She wheeled ever nearer,
Her keen gaze never faltering from her prey,
When a cloud monster surrounded her,
Snatched her up in its claws.
And the sun's rays caressed my face,
And the world was clean and new.

Shielding my eyes,
I watched,
I waited,
Then I saw her.
Again a scrap of black velvet
As she escaped the cloud monster.
Becoming ever smaller,
Farther away.
Then she was gone.
And on days when the snow drifts high
Outside my window,
I sit by the fire,
Recalling the Zephyr Queen.
And I remember that
The sun's rays caressed my face,
And the world was clean and new.

Notes

Summarize
and Synthesize

#50470 Successful Strategies

Summarize and Synthesize

Introduction

Once students have attempted or mastered the ability to find the main idea and supporting details of a text, they are ready to learn to summarize and paraphrase the nonfiction material that they read. Summarizing and paraphrasing require the development and use of a variety of skills. First, require that students use critical thinking strategies to both understand the content of what they read and also extract the essential elements of a passage. They must then be able to express the content in a way that is understandable to themselves and their readers.

Second, paraphrasing requires that students use vocabulary skills. In order to paraphrase material, they must understand crucial words. They also must have a good grasp of synonyms or know where to find them. Additionally, they need to use what they know about syntax, or sentence structure, to rewrite an author's sentences in new ways that avoid plagiarism.

Summarizing materials can help students retain information. The skill of summarizing can also be used to understand the argument that an author is trying to make or to compare and contrast points of view either within a single piece or between two pieces of writing. It can also help students grasp complicated scientific processes or social movements as they pull together a collection of thoughts.

What Is Summarizing?

Summarizing briefly recounts the important points in a piece of text. Both fiction and nonfiction can be summarized, but for the purposes of this book, only summarizing as it pertains to nonfiction will be addressed. The basic steps of a summary are to think about the main idea or message of the text and then recall the most important ideas that the author made in the text using a web, note cards, or bullets. Finally, the summary is written. Unless there is a specific reason to include an author's opinion, an important requirement of a summary is that it is based only on facts. In this way the reader can draw his or her own conclusion based on the facts presented.

What Is Synthesizing?

Synthesizing involves creating something new from a variety of sources. Synthesizing information is a process of looking closely at relationships among sources and then drawing conclusions about those relationships. Synthesis is also a process of combining information to create new ideas, a new focus, or a new perspective. Synthesizing requires students to connect to prior knowledge, evaluate new information, and draw conclusions.

Summarize and Synthesize

What Is Paraphrasing?

Paraphrasing is the act of putting someone else's words into one's own words. Although the ideas may come from someone else, paraphrasing allows a reader to repeat the ideas in an original way. Paraphrasing is not the same as quoting the source material in its initial form. In fact, paraphrasing can be better than quoting, especially when a passage is not particularly noteworthy or well written. For this reason, students need to use many synonyms and transitional words to help them paraphrase material effectively.

Being able to restate information in one's own words is a critical skill. Begin by having students preview the text for important information. As they read, have them take notes about information related to the topics or concepts they are studying. Finally, have them put their notes away and restate the most important information in their own words.

Selecting Significant Text Information

After students preview the text and delve into the reading, it is essential that they know how to recognize important information. Remind them to pay particular attention to the following text features:

- headings and subheadings
- boldfaced words
- italicized words
- captions
- illustrations
- photographs
- charts
- graphs
- maps
- labels

Model how to ask questions in order to identify significant text information. The following questions will help students focus on the text:

- What are the key concepts and/or main ideas?
- What are the important facts?
- How does the information I am reading connect to what I am learning in class?
- How do the text features help me understand what's significant?

Summarize and Synthesize

Preserving the Author's Perspective

In order to preserve the author's perspective when summarizing or paraphrasing, it is important to identify his or her point of view. Use the following questions to guide discussions:

- What is the author's perspective, or point of view, on the topic?
- How can I determine the author's perspective? Is it implicit or explicit?
- What valuable information have I learned by preserving the author's perspective?

Organizing Information

There are many ways for students to organize the information that they encounter. Some of the more traditional approaches include outlining and using note cards. It is important to teach students how to use traditional approaches, but it is also important to show them other techniques that cater to the diverse learning styles in your classroom. Some of these techniques include graphic organizers, such as double-entry journals and Venn diagrams. Given the amount of information that students will encounter over the course of their education, it is essential that they have tools for sorting information, which will help them with summarizing and paraphrasing.

Using Strategies Independently

Extensive teacher modeling of the following strategies will help students understand how to summarize and paraphrase. All strategies should be done as a whole group and then with a partner several times before letting students work independently. Be sure to model strategies in a variety of content areas, including math.

Strategy 1: Summarizing through Drawing

To get students started with the skill of summarizing, give them the definition of summarizing: relating the most important information to a given audience. Read students a short piece of nonfiction and tell them to think about the most important information. Then give students a blank sheet of paper and have them draw a picture of the key ideas in the text. Tell them that they can be as creative as they want and that they can use captions or labels, but they are not to write a paragraph. When they are finished, have them share their artistic creations with the class. On the overhead or board, keep track of students' ideas and look for commonalities among their understandings of what is most important in a text. (Standards 5.4, 7.3)

Summarize and Synthesize

Strategy 2: Writing Summaries

Writing summaries requires critical thinking. Students first need to find the main idea and the supporting details. Then they must condense the author's ideas. Finally, they must be concise, writing as much information as the reader needs in as few words and sentences as possible. (Standards 5.5, 7.3)

Select a nonfiction paragraph or section of a class textbook and use the following steps to teach summary writing:

Step 1: Read the Material

Tell students to carefully read the material to be summarized. They should think about the author's main idea as they read. What ideas does the author return to repeatedly?

Step 2: Reread the Material and Make Notes

Have students skim the material quickly. They may jot down key words and phrases on a separate sheet of paper. If the text is long, they may wish to have a separate note card for each section that they will be summarizing.

Step 3: Put the Material Aside

Direct students to close the article or textbook and begin thinking about how they want to summarize the author's ideas. They should write the author's main idea in a sentence or two and then look over their notes for information they wish to include. They can expand the notes they have made into complete sentences.

Step 4: Write the Summary

Next, students are to organize their expanded sentences into a summary. Summaries may be as brief as three sentences or as long as a page, depending on the length of the article, chapter, or book that they read. They can use the main idea to guide their organization. They might also want to think about the type of text they read. Is it a description? Does it cover a chronological period? In addition, certain transitional words such as *in addition, as a result, however, for example, first, later,* and *also* can help them tie together the ideas contained in their summary.

Step 5: Check Your Work

Have students look over their completed summaries and then return to the original material. Did they capture what the author was trying to say? Is there any information that was left out or that is not needed? Ask students to rewrite their summaries as needed.

After you have them practice summarizing a passage, distribute page 246, which gives them a seven-step plan for writing a summary. Students can keep it to use as a reference.

Summarize and Synthesize

Strategy 3: Outlining

Outlines help students organize their notes and portray hierarchical relationships. To help students understand how an outline relates to expository text, provide a nonfiction passage with the important words and phrases at the bottom of the page. Provide a second page with the appropriate Roman numerals, capital letters, and Arabic numbers. Then read the passage and complete the outline as a whole group or have students work in pairs. Use the Outlining template (page 247) for practice with this strategy. (Standards 7.3, 7.4) The following example on Komodo dragons can be used for this activity:

Komodo Dragons

Komodo dragons are one of the world's scariest animals. They are the biggest lizards in the world. They grow to be 10 feet (3 m) long and can weigh up to 300 pounds (136 kg). Their bodies have thick, dark scales that look like a knight's armor. They have sharp, jagged teeth, and claws the length of a human adult's longest finger. Dragons flick their forked tongue to smell for prey.

Besides looking terrifying, Komodo dragons are good hunters. They can run up to 10 miles per hour (16 kph) to get their prey. Then they unhinge their jaws so they can swallow pieces of meat that are bigger than their own heads. This lets them eat really big animals such as deer, wild pigs, cattle, and water buffalo. They will also eat any human being they can catch.

Komodo dragons live in burrows. They also dig deep holes in the ground to bury about two dozen eggs. After eight months the baby dragons hatch and dig themselves out of their nest. They must hide from adult dragons, including their parents, who will eat them. The babies soon learn to stay up in trees and come down only to eat. Their food is the scraps left after all the adults have finished eating.

Komodo dragons live only on Komodo Island, located between Australia and Southeast Asia. Today they are endangered because humans have wiped out much of their prey.

Important Words/Phrases

appearance	biggest lizards in the world	grow to be 10 feet long
weigh up to 300 pounds	hunters	sharp, jagged teeth
bodies	getting food	water buffalo
prey	unhinge jaws to swallow big pieces	forked tongue
thick, dark scales	long claws	baby dragons
run up to 10 miles per hour	deer	reproduction
eat adults' leftovers	wild pigs	live only on Komodo Island
Komodo dragons today	cattle	burrows
for homes	avoid adults	for eggs
hide in treetops	endangered due to humans	

Summarize and Synthesize

An outline for the passage might look like the following:

Komodo Dragons

I. Appearance
- A. Biggest lizards in the world
  1. grow to 10 feet long
  2. weigh up to 300 pounds
- B. Bodies
  1. thick, dark scales
  2. sharp, jagged teeth
  3. long claws
  4. forked tongue

II. Hunting
- A. Getting food
  1. run up to 10 miles per hour
  2. unhinge jaws to swallow big pieces
- B. Prey
  1. deer
  2. wild pigs
  3. cattle
  4. water buffalo

III. Reproduction
- A. Burrows
  1. for homes
  2. for eggs
- B. Baby Dragons
  1. avoid adults
  2. hide in treetops
  3. eat adults' leftovers

IV. Komodo dragons today
- A. live only on Komodo Island
- B. endangered due to humans

Summarize and Synthesize

Strategy 4: Summary Frame

A summary frame can help students write a personalized summary. Provide students with copies of the Summary Frame (page 248). Have them write their individual responses after the "knew" statement. Next, have them read the text and then complete the frame. (Standards 5.6, 7.3) For example:

Before I started reading about the Black Plague, I knew it was a fatal disease that had killed much of the European population. People knew little about germs or sanitary conditions.

In the article I learned that the Plague occurred during 1347–1351 and killed 50,000 people in Paris alone. Nobody knows the exact death toll because records weren't kept, but an estimated one third of Europe's whole population perished.

I also learned it was caused by a germ carried by the fleas that lived on rats.

I was surprised to find out that right before the Plague began, people had killed off most of the cats, believing that they were satanic. Since the cats had kept the rat population in check, this meant that there were more rats than ever. If there had only been more cats, the Plague would not have been as bad.

Strategy 5: Using the 5 Ws + H

The 5 Ws + H strategy can help students focus on what is important. Students can use the double-entry journal for 5 Ws + H (page 249) to record key information from the text and to write a summary using this information. Another way to have students use this strategy is to divide them into groups of four to six and assign each member of the group one of the 5 Ws + H. This variation forces them to focus on one element of the text as they are reading. Have them fill out a graphic organizer together when they are finished reading and share their information. (Standards 7.3, 8.2)

When?   **How?**   **Why?**

What?   **Who?**   **Where?**

Strategy 6: Key-Word Note Taking

Key-word note taking (page 250) is a way for students to read for important information, create a study guide, and practice summarizing at the same time. Students record key words (sometimes with a verb) on the left side of the note-taking form. Then, on the right side, they convert the key word(s) into a statement. Model how to make these statements from a passage or article. After students have completed this graphic organizer, show them how to use it as a study guide. Model how to fold the graphic organizer on the line that divides the left side from the right side. Have students quiz themselves on the summaries for each of the key words. Then show them how to turn the study guide over and quiz themselves on the key words that match the summaries. Students can work independently or with a partner to study this information. One of the benefits of this technique is that it builds students' independence in mastering their own learning. (Standards 7.3, 7.4)

The following example from a chapter in a textbook demonstrates this strategy:

Chapter 16: Pollution

pollution is (page 41)	Pollution is damage done to the earth created by waste. Pollution can hurt plants, animals, and humans.
pollution affects (page 42)	Pollution affects land, air, and water.
types of pollution (pages 41–43)	There are five kinds of pollution: • solid waste (trash, litter, junk) • air pollution (gases, smoke, chemicals, acid rain) • land pollution (chemicals, nuclear waste, solid waste) • water pollution (heat, chemicals, solid waste) • noise pollution (lots of loud sounds)
global warming (page 44)	Global warming means that the earth is warming up because there's too much carbon dioxide in the atmosphere. The carbon dioxide comes from cars, homes, and factories that burn gas, oil, and coal.

Summarize and Synthesize

Strategy 7: Topic and Detail Summary Writing

Another graphic organizer that helps students summarize is the Topic and Detail Summary Writing template (page 251). This activity requires them to identify the topic and the important details and then use that information to write a short summary. (Standards 5.1, 7.3)

Strategy 8: Paraphrasing

Paraphrasing, or rewriting material using other words, is a skill that requires modeling by the teacher and extensive practice by students. To begin teaching paraphrasing, use the Paraphrasing activity (page 252), which takes students through the steps of the process by focusing on one sentence. The following activity (page 253) explains the rules for paraphrasing—what to do and what not to do. (Standard 7.3)

Strategy 9: Paraphrasing and Vocabulary

Paraphrasing requires students to understand crucial words, have a knowledge of synonyms, and use a thesaurus. Two activities, Paraphrasing and New Vocabulary (page 254) and Paraphrasing and Vocabulary—Using a Thesaurus (page 255), can help them understand the importance of knowing the meanings of words. (Standards 5.3, 7.3)

Strategy 10: Practice with Paraphrasing

Students need to practice the difficult skill of paraphrasing. The Practice with Paraphrasing activity (page 256) takes common proverbs and asks students to rewrite them in their own words while keeping the meanings intact. You might want to model how to paraphrase by doing the first one or two or have the whole group do the first two together. (Standard 7.3)

Strategy 11: Paraphrase Passport

This strategy will help students develop their listening skills as well as their paraphrasing skills. Pair each student with a partner. One partner asks a question. Partner two answers the question. Partner one restates in his or her own words partner two's answer. Partner two decides whether his or her answer has been correctly paraphrased. The partners switch roles. (Standards 7.3, 8.2)

Here are some sentence starters to help with the paraphrasing:

Let me see if I understand what you are saying…

If I hear you correctly, you are identifying…

What you are telling me is…

Summarize and Synthesize

Writing Summaries

A summary is a condensed version of a paragraph, chapter, article, or book. Summaries can serve several purposes. They can simply retell descriptive or chronological information or give a brief rundown of a process. They also can give an overview of an author's argument by explaining the author's main idea and important points.

When you write a summary, you will need to do quite a bit of thinking. You will need to think about the author's main idea and the supporting details. You will also need to know how to paraphrase, or rewrite, the author's words in as brief a form as possible.

Summaries can be as short as a sentence or as long as a page or two, depending on the length of the material that you need to summarize.

Here are the seven steps to writing a summary:

Step 1: Read the material carefully.

Think about the main idea of what you are reading. Identify the most important supporting details or facts. Make sure that you understand the author's argument or conclusion.

Step 2: Reread the material.

As you read, think about the text type. Also, use the text organizers such as subheadings to help you organize your thinking about the material. You need to include information from each section of what you read. You may want to jot down any important points or key words and phrases that you would like to include in your summary.

Step 3: Write the main idea.

This will help you stay focused on the information to include in your summary.

Step 4: Write summary sentences.

Write a sentence that tells about each section of what you read.

Step 5: Write a draft of your summary.

Look over the main idea, key words and phrases, and sentences that you wrote. Now write a summary that gives the basic information that the reader needs to know. You do not need to include all the supporting details in your summary. Just tell the reader a few of the most important facts.

Step 6: Check your information.

Look over the original material that you read. Did you include only the most important points? Did you leave out anything that the reader should know?

Step 7: Rewrite your summary.

Read your work. It should read smoothly. Add transitional words when necessary.

Summarize and Synthesize

Outlining

Directions: Outline the passage or article you are reading. If you need more numbers or letters, use the back of this page.

Topic: _____

I. _____
   A. _____
      1. _____
      2. _____
   B. _____
      1. _____
      2. _____

II. _____
   A. _____
      1. _____
      2. _____
   B. _____
      1. _____
      2. _____

III. _____
   A. _____
      1. _____
      2. _____
   B. _____
      1. _____
      2. _____

IV. _____
   A. _____
      1. _____
      2. _____
   B. _____
      1. _____
      2. _____

Summarize and Synthesize

Summary Frame

Directions: Before you begin reading, fill in the first frame. After reading, fill in the other frames.

Before I started reading about _____, I knew _____

_____

_____

_____

- -

In the article, I learned _____

_____

_____

_____

_____

_____

- -

I also learned_____

_____

_____

_____

- -

I was surprised that_____

_____

_____

_____

_____

_____

Summarize and Synthesize

Using the 5 Ws + H

Directions: Read the text and identify the 5 Ws + H on the left side of the double-entry journal. Then write a summary on the right side.

5 Ws + H	Summary of 5 Ws + H
Who:	
What:	
Where:	
When:	
Why:	
How:	

Summarize and Synthesize

Key-Word Note Taking

Directions: Record key words with page numbers in the left column. In the right column, convert the key words into two statements.

Topic: _____

Key words & page #s	Statements
	1. 2.
	1. 2.
	1. 2.
	1. 2.

Summarize and Synthesize

Topic and Detail Summary Writing

Directions: Identify the topic and important details from the text and then use the information to write a summary.

Topic:
Important details: 1. 2. 3.

Directions: Use the information above to write a summary that clearly does the following:

- includes the important facts in your own words
- combines facts where possible
- excludes extraneous information

_____

_____

_____

_____

_____

_____

_____

_____

_____

Summarize and Synthesize

Paraphrasing—A Step-by-Step Model

To paraphrase means to rewrite material in either another form or other words. Paraphrasing is a useful skill for several reasons. You can use it when you write reports and need to retell facts. Paraphrasing prevents you from plagiarizing or stealing someone else's words. Also, when you are able to paraphrase words, you show that you understand the idea or meaning of what you have read.

Directions: Complete the following steps in paraphrasing.

1. Be sure that you understand all of the vocabulary words in the material that you are going to paraphrase. For example, read the following sentence:

   Eleanor Roosevelt was a true humanitarian and a friend to the poor and oppressed.

   Do you know the meaning of the words "humanitarian" and "oppressed"? Define the words on the lines below.

   humanitarian: _____

   oppressed: _____

2. Think about the important parts of the sentence—the subject, verb, and object. Write these on the lines below.

   subject: _____

   verb: _____

   object: _____

3. Now think about some synonyms for the words "humanitarian" and "oppressed."

   synonyms for "humanitarian": _____

   synonyms for "oppressed": _____

4. There are also phrases in a sentence to be avoided when paraphrasing so as not to plagiarize. For example, even if you find a synonym for "humanitarian," you would not want to use the adjective "true" in front of it. Do you see another phrase to avoid? Write it below.

   _____

5. Finally, paraphrase the sentence about Eleanor Roosevelt in your own words using your synonyms and new language.

   _____

Extension: Can you think of two additional ways to paraphrase the sentence?

_____

_____

Summarize and Synthesize

Paraphrasing—Do's and Don'ts

Many students wrongly believe that they can just substitute a word or two in a sentence in order to paraphrase it. The problem with substituting is that it still counts as plagiarism, or the stealing of someone else's words. In order to paraphrase correctly, follow these guidelines.

- Do think of or look up synonyms for as many words as you can, not just unusual ones.

- Do change the order of the words in the sentence.

- Do put aside the work you are paraphrasing so you are not tempted to copy it.

- Do write the paraphrase a few different ways and choose the best one.

- Do copy the original sentence or sentences onto separate paper and then edit them with proofreader's marks in order to change their meaning.

Follow these important "Don'ts" as well.

- Don't change the meaning of the original sentence or paragraph because you did not understand it.

- Don't add your own ideas to the author's or change the author's ideas.

- Don't use synonyms that do not quite fit the author's meaning.

- Don't say more or less than the author meant to say.

Directions: Now try writing the following sentences in two or three different ways. Look up any vocabulary about which you are unclear. Use synonyms that you either know or have looked up in a thesaurus. Remember to think about the author's meaning.

1. Many arctic animals survive winter by burying themselves in the ground before it freezes.

   _____

   _____

   _____

2. Moose and deer spend the day grazing in the coniferous forest.

   _____

   _____

3. Since food for animals is abundant in the deciduous forest, there is also an abundance of animal life.

   _____

   _____

   _____

Summarize and Synthesize

Paraphrasing and New Vocabulary

Directions: In order to be able to paraphrase a sentence or paragraph, you must understand any new vocabulary words that you find. When you understand all vocabulary words in the sentence, it becomes a much easier task to rewrite it. Each of the sentences below has difficult vocabulary in it for you to define. Then, after defining the words, rewrite the sentence so that it still makes sense. Use a separate sheet of paper for your work.

1. It wasn't until the 1880s that scientists recognized that the study of fossilized animal life could trace the evolutionary history of extinct species.

   Vocabulary words: fossilized, evolutionary, extinct, species

2. All dinosaurs walked with an erect posture unlike that of reptiles.

   Vocabulary words: erect, posture

3. Fossils are formed when an organism is buried in mud or sand before the hard parts of its body decay.

   Vocabulary words: organism, decay

4. Like the giant dragonfly, all invertebrate animals grew very large in prehistoric times.

   Vocabulary words: invertebrate, prehistoric

5. There are several rudimentary differences between endothermic and ectothermic animals.

   Vocabulary words: rudimentary, endothermic, ectothermic

6. Some reptiles have skin that changes due to fear, as well as fluctuations in light, humidity, and temperature.

   Vocabulary words: fluctuations, humidity

7. Due to its scarcity, an albino snake can command as much as $20,000 from its owner.

   Vocabulary words: scarcity, albino, command

8. Herpetologists conduct their studies in many different habitats.

   Vocabulary words: herpetologists, conduct, habitats

9. In spite of the extreme conditions in the desert, animal life is abundant and varied.

   Vocabulary words: extreme, abundant, varied

10. A reptile's scales act as a moisture barrier that prevents the reptile from dehydrating.

    Vocabulary words: barrier, dehydrating

Summarize and Synthesize

Paraphrasing and Vocabulary—Using a Thesaurus

A thesaurus is a book of synonyms. Several different thesauruses are published, and some are more user-friendly than others. At the bottom of this sheet, you will even find some resources for thesauruses on the Internet. A thesaurus can be especially helpful when you are trying to paraphrase someone else's work. It can help you express the new ideas you have learned from your nonfiction reading in your own way.

There are some disadvantages to using a thesaurus. One is that you can come to depend on it. When you need to substitute a word, first try to think of a new word on your own. Another problem is that you need to pick words from the thesaurus that sound like language you would use. Try to choose words that you would naturally use; otherwise, the word may stand out from the rest of your writing and stop your reader's flow of thought.

Directions: Look up the following words in a thesaurus and write some synonyms you find. On a separate sheet of paper, write a sentence using one of the synonyms.

1. dark: _____

2. follow: _____

3. sad: _____

4. nice: _____

5. polite: _____

6. dry: _____

7. brittle: _____

8. scary: _____

9. fearful: _____

10. tame: _____

11. brave: _____

12. small: _____

Internet Resources

http://thesaurus.reference.com: This site is an online version of *Roget's Thesaurus*.

http://www.m-w.com/dictionary.htm: This is the *Merriam-Webster* online edition of the *Collegiate Thesaurus*.

http://www.wordsmyth.net/home.php: This site is a complete dictionary that includes synonyms.

Summarize and Synthesize

Practice with Paraphrasing

Directions: Read each proverb below and discuss its meaning with your classmates. Then paraphrase the proverbs. Paraphrasing proverbs and sayings can provide good practice with this skill. Remember that to *paraphrase* means to rewrite an author's words in your own words while still keeping the author's meaning.

1. A penny saved is a penny earned._____

2. You can catch more flies with honey than with vinegar. _____

_____

3. The only things certain in life are death and taxes. _____

_____

4. Finders, keepers; losers, weepers._____

5. Make hay while the sun shines. _____

6. Birds of a feather flock together. _____

7. Let sleeping dogs lie._____

8. All's well that ends well._____

9. Don't count your chickens before they hatch. _____

10. Haste makes waste. _____

11. An apple a day keeps the doctor away._____

12. Great minds think alike. _____

13. Too many cooks spoil the broth._____

14. A watched pot never boils. _____

15. A stitch in time saves nine. _____

16. Loose lips sink ships. _____

17. A journey of a thousand miles begins with a single step. _____

_____

18. You can lead a horse to water, but you can't make it drink. _____

_____

19. Home is where the heart is._____

20. Beauty is in the eye of the beholder._____

Passport to Comprehension

Developing Vocabulary

Developing Vocabulary

Introduction

Most teachers know that rote memorization of vocabulary words is ineffective for expanding students' word knowledge. Students need to understand new words that they encounter in their reading if their knowledge base is to increase. In addition to learning word meanings in context, students also need skills to break down words in order to approach their reading with independence and confidence.

Nonfiction reading especially requires the ability to understand technical language. Science and social studies demand that students recognize and build their vocabularies. Mathematics also has a specialized language that students must learn if they are to advance.

Teaching vocabulary can be a frustrating experience if teachers do not have a plan other than assigning a list of words for students to define with a glossary or dictionary. Allot instructional time to word study. Students need to learn not only the meaning of words but also their applicability. In other words, once students learn a new term, they can think about other contexts in which the term might be used and in this way enhance their understanding of that term. When beginning to read an interesting chapter or book, students are easily drawn into the material. Time spent on word study at the outset, however, will pay off handsomely as students will better comprehend the material and begin to use the vocabulary independently.

In short, Abbott (1999) states that vocabulary development should help students become adept at using a variety of word-recognition strategies; unlock meanings of technical and specialized words in each content area; establish a systematic, lifelong method of vocabulary inquiry; and become motivated and enthusiastic about vocabulary study.

Selecting Vocabulary Words to Study

Many teachers feel overwhelmed when teaching vocabulary because they realize that it is impossible to thoroughly cover all unknown words. Do not attempt to teach every unknown word. Instead, choose words from each selection wisely. Following these guidelines will result in an educationally sound vocabulary list:

- First, choose words that are critical to the article's meaning.

- Then, choose conceptually difficult words.

- Finally, choose words with the greatest utility—those that you anticipate students will see more often (e.g., choose "anxious" rather than "appalled").

If you prefer to give students a sense of control over their own learning, you can have them choose the words to be studied. First, put students into teams of three. Have them read the passage and decide as a group which three words they would like to study. When you reconvene as a class, each team tells you the three words it selected. Record their responses on the board, overhead, or chart paper. Do not record any word more than once. Once the list is established, have students define any terms that they can and look up the meanings of the others in the dictionary. Write the definition next to each term and have students copy all the information into their class notebooks.

Developing Vocabulary

Elements of Effective Vocabulary Instruction

A wide variety of techniques, as outlined in this section, is essential for successful vocabulary development. Research has shown that the most effective vocabulary program utilizes contextual, structural, and classification strategies. Vocabulary instruction is only effective if students permanently add the concepts to their knowledge base. You can achieve success by making certain that your vocabulary instruction includes the following elements:

- using context clues

- knowing the meaning of affixes (prefixes, suffixes) and roots

- learning synonyms and antonyms

- categorizing (sorting) and classifying concepts

Using Context Clues

Learning vocabulary in context is important for two reasons. First, it makes students become active in determining word meanings; and second, it offers them a way to figure out unknown words in their independent reading. If you teach students how to use context clues, you will eventually be able to omit pre-teaching any vocabulary that is defined in context (as long as the text is written at students' independent reading levels).

There are five basic kinds of context clues:

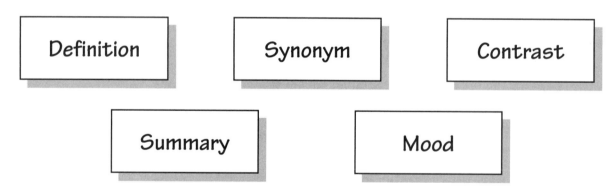

1. **Definition:** The easiest case occurs when the definition is given elsewhere in the sentence or paragraph.

   Example: The ragged, bedraggled dress hung from her shoulders.

Developing Vocabulary

Using Context Clues *(cont.)*

2. **Synonym:** Another simple case occurs when a synonym or synonymous phrase is immediately used.

   Example: The room was so dank that you could feel the dampness creep into your clothing.

3. **Contrast:** The meaning may be implied through contrast to a known word or concept. Be alert to these words that signal contrast: "although," "but," "however," "even though."

   Example: Clothes purchased off a department store rack will rarely be mistaken for haute couture.

4. **Summary:** Another form is a summary that provides a list of attributes.

   Example: Tundra, desert, grassland, and rain forest are the names of four of Earth's biomes.

5. **Mood:** Sometimes the meaning can be grasped from the mood of the larger context in which it appears. In the most difficult situation the meaning must be inferred with few other clues.

   Example: In America, the end of World War II was marked by a wild sense of euphoria. People were singing and dancing in the streets, many businesses gave their workers the day off with pay, and almost every city nationwide had huge fireworks displays and parades.

   Example: Her shrill voice was actually making my ears hurt.

Words in Context

When students can define words in context, their comprehension levels will increase. Secondary-level students should be proficient in using context to gain a clear sense of the concepts they are exploring, the topics they are studying, and the purpose for their learning. Structured discussions, small-group dialogues, and paired readings will build students' abilities to identify words in context because they will hear their teacher and classmates use unknown words in real-life conversations. When proficient readers encounter a word they don't know, they ask three questions:

- Do I know this word?

- If so, how do I know this word? If not, how can I learn this word?

- Do I need to know this word?

Proficient readers answer these questions by using context, activating prior knowledge, and using resources available to them. Struggling readers have great difficulty using context and need highly structured word-attack strategies in order to make sense of unknown words.

Developing Vocabulary

Word and Sentence Meanings

Students must be exposed to a variety of texts in all content areas. In each subject, students must be taught how to read sentences to determine word meaning. When using various techniques to make sense of words in context, students should consider the following word-attack strategies:

1. Reread the sentence to try to understand the word based on sentence meaning.

2. Use the dictionary to find a definition that makes sense within the context of the sentence.

3. Reread the previous sentence.

4. Go on and read the next sentence.

5. Ask the teacher or a friend to read the sentence to you.

6. Look for key words in the sentence that may reveal the word's meaning.

7. Stop reading and think about what makes sense.

8. Look for pictures near the word or sentence to see if they help you understand.

9. Think about whether you need to know the word. Skip it if you can figure out what the sentence means without knowing the word.

Root Words

One of the main factors of acquiring vocabulary knowledge in students is their growing awareness and proficiency with root words, suffixes, and prefixes. *Morphology* is the ability to use word structures to make meaning of new vocabulary. Explicit instruction that teaches students how to use their prior knowledge to make sense of root words, suffixes, and prefixes will result in growing confidence in understanding words and ultimately an increase in reading comprehension. Some key questions will help students with using morphology.

1. What is the root word? What prior knowledge do I have to help me define this word?

2. What is the prefix? What does it mean? How does it change the root word?

3. What is the suffix? What does it mean? How does it change the root word?

4. How does knowing parts of words help me understand the meaning of new words?

The Root Words activity (page 268) gives students practice with unlocking word meaning.

Developing Vocabulary

Interpreting Words with Multiple Meanings

Since many words have multiple meanings, students need to have ways to discern when a familiar word does not make sense in the context of the sentence. Often students will encounter a word being used differently because it has another definition with which they are unfamiliar. Often, words are also used differently based on the subject area. For example, in math the word "change" means money. In science, "change" is connected to catalysts and experimentation. In social studies, "change" is connected to politics, history, and economics. A helpful technique for teaching the concept of multiple meanings is to create a large comparison chart that shows how words are used differently in each subject area. Make multiple copies of the chart so different content-area teachers can add to the chart during the school year, showing students how words are used differently across the content areas.

Identifying Shades of Meaning

When students are able to understand the shades of meaning of words, they will gain deeper levels of comprehension. The ability to interpret different meanings of words is particularly useful when learning key concepts such as conflict, change, freedom, and symmetry. At the secondary-school level, it is particularly beneficial for teachers to plan interdisciplinary lessons in which concepts and key vocabulary are discussed with particular attention paid to shades of meaning. Students will be able to make connections among major concepts and link facts to concepts when they explore multiple meanings.

Understanding Denotative and Connotative Meanings

By the time students reach the secondary level, it is important for them to know the difference between denotative and connotative meanings. Remind them that denotative meaning is the dictionary definition of a word. Connotative meanings are the secondary implications or associated meanings of a word. Being able to connote meaning is a challenging task that requires the reader to understand the set of attributes that constitutes the meaning of a term.

Understanding Words Related to Content Areas

Students need to know the technical vocabulary for various content areas in order to better understand and acquire content knowledge. For example, in science, students should have mastery of certain words such as "experiment," "scientific method," "theory," "hypothesis," "catalyst," and "conclusion." Proficiency with such content-specific vocabulary will lead to greater facility with learning facts and increase students' abilities to synthesize and evaluate information.

Developing Vocabulary

Using Dictionaries and Other Reference Materials

While it is important to teach students how to identify the meanings of words in context and to use other text-based strategies, it is also important to give them continued practice with using dictionaries and other reference materials. Give them the opportunity to find word meanings by organizing individual and group games, such as scavenger hunts. Assign students content-specific vocabulary and have them use the guide words at the top of the pages of the dictionary to find the word. Then have them identify the word's meaning, part of speech, and root.

Using Strategies Independently

Modeling how to define words in context, activate prior knowledge, and use available resources will provide the foundation for students to use vocabulary strategies independently. Remember to have students engage in whole-class discussion, small-group activities, and paired reading in order to gain a greater facility with vocabulary through structured instruction and socialization. Gradually release the responsibility for learning new vocabulary based on your assessment of their readiness and independence.

Strategy 1: Contextual Defining

Struggling readers may have difficulty using context clues so it is important that they are presented with highly structured approaches to making meaning of words through context. Use the Contextual Defining activity (page 269) to have them identify the unknown word, copy the sentence in which it is used, and write an explanation of the context. Then expose students to contextual understandings from the teacher and a partner. Also, have them create their own sentences using the word. All students will benefit from this process, but struggling readers will benefit most through the structured support of their teachers and classmates. (Standards 5.3, 7.4)

The following example shows how to use this strategy:

Vocabulary word: *dispute*

Context from the text	Context from the teacher
The driver had a *dispute* with the police officer after he was pulled over for speeding.	The restaurant customer had a *dispute* with the waiter when he charged the customer for something she did not order.
Context from you (the student)	**Context from a partner**
My mom and dad had a *dispute* when we ran out of gas on the way to school.	I had a *dispute* with my friend when she wouldn't share the ball with me.

Dictionary definition: A *dispute* is a disagreement or argument.

Developing Vocabulary

Strategy 2: Charting Characteristics

Charting key characteristics is a good technique for identifying attributes related to a particular set of terms. The Charting Characteristics activity (page 270) will help with this process. For example, if students were studying mammals in a science class, they would record the mammals in the left-hand column (mice, gorillas, cats, dogs, sheep, elephants, etc.). Across the top of the chart they would record various characteristics, such as carnivorous, herbivorous, omnivorous, domestic, wild, friendly, unfriendly, travels in packs, travels independently, etc. Students would read the information about the mammals and place a check in the box that corresponds with the particular characteristic that was confirmed in the text. (Standards 5.3, 5.5)

Strategy 3: Personal Association Vocabulary Strategy

When students make sense of vocabulary words by applying them to their own lives, there is a greater likelihood that they will retain the definitions in their long-term memories. For this strategy, students identify the vocabulary word and draw a simple illustration or symbolic representation of the word. Then they list their personal associations with the word. For example, if the word is "triangulate," students may focus on the prefix "tri" and associate it with tricycle, triathlon, tripod, and trident. They may notice that all of these words have something to do with the number 3. After some discussion with a peer group or a partner over the meaning of the word, students may look up the word in a dictionary. Then have them generate a list of examples and non-examples of the word based on their personal experiences. Use the Personal Association Vocabulary Strategy activity (page 271) for this strategy. (Standards 5.3, 7.4)

Strategy 4: Vocabulary Explorations through Questioning

Model this strategy by identifying an unknown word and asking students four questions to help them reflect on using the word, connecting it to personal experience, teaching the word to someone else, and encountering the word again. Use the questions from the Vocabulary Explorations through Questioning activity (page 272). Then distribute the activity and have students use it as they read the text. The following is an example of this strategy for the word "adjacent." (Standards 5.3, 8.2)

Unusual or unknown word: _adjacent_	
Questions heard	**Responses**
How would you use this vocabulary word in your writing or everyday conversation?	My house is adjacent to a park.
How does this vocabulary word connect to your personal experience or prior knowledge?	I have heard my mom give directions to our house and use the word "adjacent" when she tells someone we live next to the park.
How would you teach this vocabulary word to someone else?	I would tell them it means "next to" or "beside something" and then give them examples.
Where would you expect to encounter this word in the future?	I might see the word "adjacent" when a location or direction of something is being described.

Developing Vocabulary

Strategy 5: Text Coding and Vocabulary

Tell students that they will be focusing on vocabulary in their reading. Present them with the following codes:

**	=	Important
?	=	I don't understand
??	=	I wonder…
✓	=	This word connects to the concept because…

These codes will help them focus on important words, words they don't understand or wonder about, and words that connect with the concept they are studying. Have them write directly in the text or use sticky notes to record their codes. When they finish reading, they can use the Text Coding and Vocabulary activity (page 273) to record the vocabulary words that they coded and to reflect on the words' meanings by using the sentence starters. (Standards 5.3, 5.6)

Strategy 6: Capsule Vocabulary

Originally developed by Crist (1975) and further explained by Judith Irvin (1990), capsule vocabulary incorporates listening, speaking, reading, and writing into the process of learning new vocabulary. Begin by preparing a "capsule" of vocabulary words related to the topic. This capsule could be a real container that holds the words, or you could draw a large picture of a capsule on the board and "fill" it with the vocabulary words by writing them in the drawing. Next, engage students in an extended discussion in which you use the capsule vocabulary words to discuss the topic. Then have students use the Capsule Vocabulary activity (page 274) to record the words, have a group conversation using the words, listen to the teacher and record the words, write a mini-story or description using the words, and read the text, recording the number of times those words appear. (Standards 5.3, 7.3)

Strategy 7: Personification Vocabulary

With this strategy, students define unknown vocabulary words and then personify those words. For example, if a student were to personify the word "lovely," he or she might write: "Lovely walks down the street carrying a bundle of roses while flipping her luxurious chestnut-colored hair over her shoulders." Or if a student were to personify the word "hideous," he or she might write: "Hideous likes to hide in old gnarled trees and growl loudly while picking his teeth and scratching his head covered with greasy black hair." Use the Personification Vocabulary activity (page 275) for this strategy. (Standards 5.3, 7.4)

Developing Vocabulary

Strategy 8: Exploring Content Vocabulary

When students are studying a complicated or difficult concept, they need to focus on those words that are particularly troublesome. An effective strategy requires them to focus on one word at a time, asking why they need to know the word, how it connects to other words, which is the most challenging word, and which word is difficult to pronounce. These questions help them identify specific problems they are having with comprehending the material. Also, the Exploring Content Vocabulary activity (page 276) can help teachers identify students' trouble spots for re-teaching. (Standards 5.3, 5.4)

Strategy 9: Dictionary Definitions

To give students practice with looking up words in the dictionary, use the Dictionary Definitions activity (page 277). To vary this process, you can assign specific difficult words that students will encounter in a lesson or text, or you can give students a blank activity and have them choose their own list of unfamiliar words as they read. This strategy can be done individually, with partners, or in small groups. (Standards 5.3, 7.2)

Strategy 10: Artistic Interpretations

To build students' understanding of new words, use drama. Divide students into groups or pairs to create a mini-skit or dramatic "photograph" illustrating their understanding of a word. If students created a dramatic photograph of the word "antagonistic," they would have a student with an angry look on his or her face, frozen in the position of preparing to punch someone. The other students would face the antagonistic student in frozen positions with terrified looks on their faces.

For an artistic variation, use the Artistic Interpretations activity (page 278) to have students identify a word, define it in context, and look it up in a dictionary. They draw an illustration of the word interacting with other ideas, people, places, or things. For example, if the word is "freedom," a student may draw a picture of a happy person holding the American flag, or the Statue of Liberty, or a bald eagle—all symbols of freedom in our country. Such a picture shows that the student understood cultural synonyms for the word "freedom." (Standards 5.3, 7.4)

Strategy 11: Vocabulary Baseball

Games are highly motivational to students. To set up vocabulary baseball, post a home base, first base, second base, and third base strategically around the classroom. Divide the class into two teams. In addition to 10 batters, each team can have a scorekeeper and coaches at every base. For the first team up at bat, "pitch" the vocabulary word to the first batter. The batter needs to define the word, use it in a sentence, and spell the word. For each part that the batter does correctly, he or she gets a base. For example, if the batter can do all three things, he or she has hit a triple. When a player cannot do any part, he or she is out. When the team has three outs, it sits down and the other team bats. If students have prepared for the game, you may not have many outs, so you may have to set a five-run limit. (Standards 5.3, 7.4)

Developing Vocabulary

Root Words

Directions: Identify the unknown words. Look up the words and record their definitions, roots, prefixes, and suffixes.

Unknown word	Definition	Root	Prefixes	Suffixes

Developing Vocabulary

Contextual Defining

Directions: Use the following four contexts to come to an understanding of the unknown word.

Vocabulary word: _____

Context from the text	Context from the teacher
Copy the sentence in which the word is found or explain the context.	Copy the sentence from the teacher in which the word is used in context.
Context from you	**Context from a partner**
Create a sentence in which you use the word in context based on the text's use and your teacher's use.	Copy the sentence that your partner wrote in which he or she applied contextual understanding.

Dictionary definition: _____

_____

How did the contextual defining exercise help you understand the word before you looked it up in the dictionary?

_____

_____

_____

Developing Vocabulary

Charting Characteristics

Directions: Record terms to be compared and the characteristics that you will analyze. As you learn about each term, place a check in the characteristics column that connects to the term.

Characteristics to be analyzed ▮▮▶					
Terms to be compared ⬇					
1.					
2.					
3.					
4.					
5.					
6.					
7.					
8.					
9.					

Developing Vocabulary

Personal Association Vocabulary Strategy

Directions: Use the following chart to make personal associations to a new vocabulary word.

Vocabulary word and illustration	Personal association(s)
Examples	**Non-examples**

Developing Vocabulary

Vocabulary Explorations through Questioning

Directions: Use the following chart to question the unusual or unknown words that you encountered in the text.

Unusual or unknown word: _____	
Questions heard	**Responses**
How would you use this vocabulary word in your writing or everyday conversation?	
How does this vocabulary word connect to your personal experience or prior knowledge?	
How would you teach this vocabulary word to someone else?	
Where would you expect to encounter this word in the future?	

Developing Vocabulary

Text Coding and Vocabulary

Directions: As you read, use the codes below to mark in the margins or on sticky notes next to specific vocabulary words. Then record the vocabulary word and elaborate on the code that you used to mark the text.

**	=	Important
?	=	I don't understand
??	=	I wonder
→	=	This word connects to the concept because…

Vocabulary word (Use the text coding to find text information.)	**Response** (Choose from the sentence starters below to get started on your response.)
	** = I think this word is important because…
	? = I don't understand this word because…
	?? = I wonder if this words means _____ because…
	→ = This word connects to the concept because…

Developing Vocabulary

Capsule Vocabulary

Directions: Record conceptually linked vocabulary words found while speaking, listening, writing, and reading.

Capsule vocabulary: words related to the topic

_____

_____

_____

_____

Have a conversation with your group and use as many capsule words as possible. Make a list of words used.

_____

_____

_____

_____

Listen to your teacher and record the capsule words that you hear him or her use.

_____

_____

_____

_____

Write a short story and use as many capsule words as possible.

_____

_____

_____

_____

Read the text and record all of the capsule words included in the text.

_____

_____

_____

_____

Personification Vocabulary

Directions: Personify the vocabulary words you are studying by giving them human traits.

Vocabulary word	Definition	Personification of vocabulary word

Developing Vocabulary

Exploring Content Vocabulary

Directions: Explore the content vocabulary connected to the topic you are studying.

Identify words that are specific to the content area that you are studying.	Choose one word. Why do you need to know this word? How will it be useful to you?
Choose a different word. How does this word connect to other words that you are learning related to this topic?	Choose yet another word. What similes or metaphors could you create using this word?
Examine all the words. Which word is the most challenging to understand? Why?	Examine all the words again. Which word is the most difficult to pronounce? Spell it phonetically in the space below.

Developing Vocabulary

Dictionary Definitions

Directions: Use the dictionary to look up unknown vocabulary words.

Unknown word	Guide words at top of page	Pronunciation	Part of speech	Definition

Developing Vocabulary

Artistic Interpretations

Directions: Identify the unknown word and use the context to write a definition. After looking up the word in a dictionary, draw a creative picture of the word. Finally, reflect on your drawing by responding to the questions at the bottom of the page.

Unknown word: _____

Definition based on context: _____

_____

Dictionary definition: _____

_____

Illustration of the word: (Draw a picture that shows the word interacting with other people, places, or things. Be creative!)

What details did you add to your picture that surprised you? What are your most creative or insightful details? How could you use this word in your own life?

_____

_____

_____

How did drawing a picture of the word help you better understand the word?

_____

_____

Works Cited

Abbott, S. 1999. *Teaching reading in the middle grades*. Huntington Beach, CA: Teacher Created Materials, Inc.

Baker, L. 2002. Metacognition in comprehension instruction. In *Comprehension instruction: Research-based best practices*, ed. C. C. Block and M. Pressley, 77–95. New York: Guilford Press.

Baker, L., and A. L. Brown. 1984. Metacognitive skills and reading. In *Handbook of reading research*, ed. P. D. Pearson, R. Barr, M. L. Kamil, and P. Mosenthal, 353–94. Mahwah, NJ: Lawrence Erlbaum.

Block, C. C. 1999. Comprehension: Crafting understanding. In *Best practices in literacy instruction*, ed. L. B. Gambrell, L. M. Morrow, S. B. Neuman, and M. Pressley, 98–118. New York: Guilford Press.

Crist, B. I. 1975. One capsule a week: A painless remedy for vocabulary ills. *Journal of Reading* 19:147–49.

Cunningham, D, and S. L. Shablak. 1975. Selective reading guide-o-rama: The content teacher's best friend. *Journal of Reading* 18 (5): 380–82.

Dole, J. A., K. J. Brown, and W. Trathen. 1996. The effects of strategy instruction on the comprehension performance of at-risk students. *Reading Research Quarterly* 31 (1): 62–88.

Duke, N. K., and P. D. Pearson. 2002. Effective practices for developing reading comprehension. In *What research has to say about reading instruction.* 3rd ed. Ed. A. E. Farstup and S. J. Samuels, 205–42. Newark, DE: International Reading Association, Inc.

Durkin, D. 1978. What classroom observations reveal about reading comprehension instruction. *Reading Research Quarterly* 14 (4): 481–533.

Enciso, P. 1992. Creating the storyworld: A case study of a young reader's engagement strategies and stances. In *Reader stance and literary understanding: Exploring the theories, research, and practice*, ed. J. Many and C. Cox, 75–102. Norwood, NJ: Ablex.

Garner, R. 1987. *Metacognition and reading comprehension*. Norwood, NJ: Ablex.

Harvey, S., and A. Goudvis. 2000. *Strategies that work*. Portland, ME: Stenhouse.

Holmes, B. C., and N. L. Roser. 1987. Five ways to assess readers' prior knowledge. *The Reading Teacher* 40 (7): 646–49.

Irvin, J. L. 1990. *Reading and the middle school student: Strategies to enhance literacy*. Needham Heights, MA: Allyn and Bacon.

Irvin, J. L. 1998. *Reading and the middle school student: Strategies to enhance literacy*. 2nd ed. Needham Heights, MA: Allyn and Bacon.

Keene, E. O. 2002. From good to memorable: Characteristics of highly effective comprehension teaching. In *Improving comprehension instruction*, ed. C. C. Block, L. B. Gambrell, and M. Pressley, 80–105. San Francisco: Jossey-Bass.

Works Cited

Kragler, S., C. A. Walker, and L. E. Martin. 2005. Strategy instruction in primary content textbooks. *The Reading Teacher* 59 (3): 254–61.

Langer, J. 1987. Envisionment: A reader-based view of comprehension. *The California Reader* 20 (3): 4–7.

Langer, J. 1991. Literacy and schooling: A sociocognitive perspective. In *Literacy for a diverse society*, ed. E. Hiebert, 9–27. New York: Teachers College Press.

Mastropieri, M. A., and T. E. Scruggs. 1997. Best practices in promoting reading comprehension in students with learning disabilities. *Remedial and Special Education* 18 (4): 197–214.

McCarthy, S., L. Hoffman, and J. Galda. 1999. Readers in elementary classrooms: Learning goals and instructional principles. In *Engaged reading*, ed. J. Guthrie and D. Alvermann, 46–80. New York: Teachers College Press.

Meichenbaum, D., B. Burland, L. Gruson, and R. Cameron. 1985. The growth of reflection in children. In *Metacognitive assessment*, ed. S. Yusson, 3–30. London: Academic Press.

National Reading Panel. 2000. *Teaching children to read: An evidence-based assessment of the scientific research literature on reading and its implications for reading instruction—reports of the subgroups.* Washington, DC: National Institute of Child Health and Human Development.

Paris, S. G., B. A. Wasik, and J. C. Turner. 1991. The development of strategic readers. In vol. 2 of *Handbook of reading research,* ed. R. Barr, M. L. Kamil, P. Mosenthal, and P. D. Pearson, 609–40. Mahwah, NJ: Lawrence Erlbaum.

Pressley, M. 2000. What should comprehension instruction be the instruction of? In vol. 3 of *Handbook of reading research,* ed. R. Barr, M. L. Kamil, P. B. Mosenthal, and P. D. Pearson, 545–62. Mahwah, NJ: Lawrence Erlbaum.

———. 2002. Metacognition and self-regulated comprehension. In *What research has to say about reading instruction*. 3rd ed. Ed. A. E. Farstrup and S. J. Samuels, 291–309. Newark, DE: International Reading Association, Inc.

Pressley, M., and P. Afflerbach. 1995. *Verbal protocols for reading: The nature of constructively responsive reading.* Hillsdale, NJ: Lawrence Erlbaum.

Raphael, T. 1982. Question-answer strategies for children. *The Reading Teacher* 36:189–90.

Robinson, F. P. 1970. *Effective study.* 4th ed. New York: Harper and Row.

Roehler, L. R., and G. G. Duffy. 1991. Teacher's instructional actions. In vol. 2 of *Handbook of reading research*, ed. R. Barr, M. L. Kamil, P. B. Mosenthal, and P. D. Pearson, 861–84. Mahwah, NJ: Lawrence Erlbaum.

Schraw, G. 1998. Promoting general metacognitive awareness. *Instructional Science* 26 (1–2): 113–25.

Vaughn, J., and T. Estes. 1986. *Reading and reasoning beyond the primary grades.* Needham Heights, MA: Allyn and Bacon.